General Fabrics Company

P.O. Box 6084,
Providence, RI 02940

(401)728-4200 FAX (401) 728-2580
Generalfabrics@genfabco.com
Showroom: 1359 Broadway, Suite 808,
New York, NY 10018

COTTON CANDY NINE PATCH SQUARED—Designed especially for beginning quilters
by Sue Pickering

General Fabrics Company's beautiful fabric group, Cotton Candy, was the inspiration for this cheerful wall hanging. Quilt designeer Sue Pickering has used all the colors of the rainbow and many fabrics to achieve the contemporary looking quilt. Customize the colors to your decorating theme. With so many Cotton Candy fabrics to choose from, you just may want some of each flavor!

QUILT SIZE	# BLOCKS	DIMENSIONS	ASSORTED FABRIC FOR TOP	BACKING & BINDING
Wall	9 set 3x3	33" x 33"	2 yards	1 1/2 yards
Crib	12 set 3x4	33" x 44"	2 1/2 yards	2 yards
Twin	48 set 6 x 8	66" x 88"	8 yards	7 1/2 yards
Double	56 set 7 x 8	77" x 88"	9 yards	8 yards
Queen	72 set 8 x 9	88" x 99"	10 yards	8 1/2 yards
King	81 set 9 x 9	99" x 99"	11 yards	10 yards

(See reverse side for instructions.)

COTTON CANDY
NINE PATCH SQUARED

Designed especially for beginning quilters
by Sue Pickering

Graphics by Doreen C. Burbank

12	6	12	9	8	9	1	4	1
6	♡2	6	8	♡6	8	4	♡13	4
12	6	12	9	8	9	1	4	1
10	3	10	15	4	15	11	7	11
3	♡7	3	4	♡3	4	7	♡5	7
10	3	10	15	4	15	11	7	11
13	4	13	9	2	9	14	5	14
4	♡9	4	2	♡8	2	5	♡3	5
13	4	13	9	2	9	14	5	14

Fabric Placement

Number	Pattern	Color	SKU #
1	7693	Green	5330808
2	7985	Green	5331012
3	7986	Green	5331178
4	7822	Blue	5331277
5	7693	Blue	5331376
6	7985	Blue	5341201
7	7822	Yellow	5341458
8	7985	Yellow	5341821
9	7822	Purple	5342076
10	7693	Purple	5342241
11	7985	Purple	5342308
12	7822	Pink	5342522
13	7693	Pink	5342639
14	7985	Pink	5342761
15	7986	Pink	5342985

Refer to the color picture on the front for one color suggestion. All yardage estimates are for total minimum yardage. However, it's best to buy backing and binding fabric now so it will match. Quarter-inch seam allowances have been included in the cutting measurements.

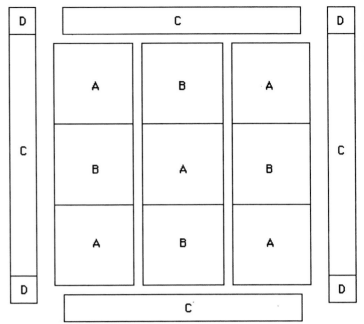

Block Assembly Diagram

To construct each block you will need to cut:
A   five 3 1/2" squares for the 9-patch
B   four 3 1/2" squares for the 9-patch
C   four 1 1/2" x 9 1/2" rectangles for sashing
D   four 1 1/2" squares for the corner posts
E   one heart—no larger than 2 1/2"—
    cut from scraps and fused or appliqued in place

For quicker cutting of A and B pieces, first cut one 3 1/2" wide strip across the fabric, then recut into 3 1/2" squares. From the fabric left over, cut 1 1/2" wide fabric strips and recut into 9 1/2" lengths for sashing (C) and 1 1/2" squares for corner posts (D).

Block construction: **All seams are 1/4".**
1. Sew the five A squares and four B squares together as shown in assembly diagram. Iron seams toward darker fabric. Match seam junctions carefully.
2. Sashing: Sew two C sashing rectangles to the top and bottom of the nine-patch, matching edges. Press after each step.
3. Sew the four small D corner post squares to the remaining two C sashing rectangles, one on each end.
5. Make the number of blocks necessary for the size of your project. See front page for number of blocks needed for the quilt size you desire.

Finishing:
Assemble the blocks in a pleasing color arrangement, carefully matching seams where necessary. Press well.

Construct backing as needed, at least 2" larger than the quilt on all sides. Sandwich the backing, cotton batting, and quilt top, and baste or safety pin in place. Machine quilt or hand quilt as you prefer. Trim the batting and backing to 1/4" from the edge of the top. Make 2" wide binding, and sew in place in your favorite manner. Now it's a quilt!

Weekend

Star Quilts

for People Who Don't Have Time to Quilt

by Marti Michell

Book V of the
"Quilting for People Who Don't Have Time to Quilt" Series

Featuring:

✦ Many Variations of
   Ohio Star or Variable Star

✦ Adaptations of Favorite
   Traditional Designs

✦ New Rotary Cutting Key
   Converts Pattern Pieces to
   Rotary Cutting

✦ Quilt-As-You-Sew Invisible
   Machine Quilting

✦ Quilt-As-You-Sew Borders and
   Finishing Methods

✦ Traditional Machine Quilting

Introduction

When you think "quilt," do you imagine a little, old lady with bleeding fingers stooped over a quilt frame? Do you assume she will be there for months?

Well, think again! The techniques presented in this book speed up all the steps, eliminating the quilt frame and the bleeding fingers, and reducing the time required to complete a quilt to hours.

With the Quilt-As-You-Sew techniques you will learn in this book, you really can complete a Star Quilt in a single weekend. However, just because the quilts can be made in a weekend, it isn't mandatory! You may prefer to spread the time needed to complete your quilt over several weekends. If you are planning to make a full-size bed quilt, it will be much more relaxed if you're lucky enough to have a three-day weekend! If you only have two days, you may want to drop any plans for cooking or movie-going.

Just What is Quilt-As-You-Sew?

The easiest way to describe Quilt-As-You-Sew is to compare it to other quiltmaking procedures. In traditional quilting, the quiltmaker pieces or appliqués each block or section, assembles the blocks into a quilt top, pins or bastes the quilt top to the batting and backing, and only then begins to quilt.

In a process called quilt-as-you-go, lap quilting or apartment quilting, the process is slightly rearranged. First the blocks are pieced; then each one is individually quilted, (eliminating the need for a full-sized quilt frame); then the quilted blocks are assembled. But the Quilt-As-You-Sew technique is even easier and faster!

With Quilt-As-You-Sew techniques, you actually quilt with some or all of the same stitching that assembles or pieces the block, and almost all of the stitching is done by machine. You will see that there are many variations of Quilt-As-You-Sew, including only attaching the borders (to traditionally-pieced quilt tops). The best thing about any Quilt-As-You-Sew method is that it results in completed quilts, not just quilt tops!

No quilt frame is needed, and no time is wasted learning how to use a quilt frame. Time-consuming hand work is reduced to a minimum. Beautiful quilts to use or share can be yours in less time than you ever dreamed.

I LOVE HAND QUILTING!

It's not that I don't like hand quilting or hand-quilted quilts, it's just that I am realistic about the amount of time that I have. The productivity of the Quilt-As-You-Sew

methods allows quilts to become easy gift items, because the amount of time invested is minimal.

If you've never made a hand-quilted quilt, you may no understand that most of the time, a person who gives hand-quilted quilt continues to refer to it as "my quilt. The quiltmaker doesn't go to visit the recipient, but t check on the quilt!

I ALSO LOVE MACHINE QUILTING

Call me fickle, but I also love machine quilting and believ it's okay for machine quilting to be seen. Sometimes, th more the machine quilting shows and sparkles wit metallic threads and becomes an integral part of the quil the happier I am.

However, in an earlier stage of my quilting life, I wouldn have dreamed of machine quilting. Eventually, the realit of the machine speed set in and I started to figure ou ways to machine quilt without letting any of the stitchin show on the top of the quilt. I went to great lengths t develop techniques for hidden machine quilting.

I'm glad I went through that period, because that wa when the basic method for Quilt-As-You-Sew surfaced and it really is a wonderful technique. At this point in m quilting, I willingly mix the hidden Quilt-As-You-Sew techniques with more visible machine quilting. The basi principle still remains, whenever a seam made for th purpose of piecing can go through the backing and battin at the same time, that is one less seam that needs to b quilted later.

FINDING SUITABLE BLOCKS

Some quilt block designs fall naturally into the Quilt-As You-Sew category. The most obvious is the Log Cabin, see **Weekend Log Cabin Quilts** (ASN book 4126). I have always been fascinated by the Log Cabin block where the pieces spiral around the center square. As it happens, the spiraling construction is what makes the block so con ducive to Quilt-As-You-Sew techniques.

With Weekend Star quilts, the Quilt-As-You-Sew tech niques are not as obvious. You have to be willing to look beyond the typical construction methods and take advan tage of pre-piecing some sub-unit sections traditionally t make the Weekend Star Quilts.

ENJOY!

Remember, there are no rules. These are quilts to make for fun, for using and for sharing. Sometimes people think some of the things I do for quiltmaking fun are unortho dox. Whenever their "but that isn't the way 'they' do it" attitude surfaces, I just think, "I don't know who 'they' are, but this is how I do it."

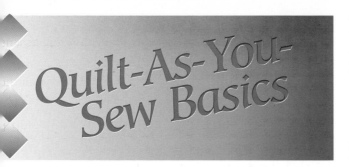

Quilt-As-You-Sew Basics

While much of the information in this section is applicable to any quilting, it has been slanted to specifically cover Quilt-As-You-Sew methods. See page 14 for general information about making these quilts using traditional techniques.

What Size Are the Quilts?

With the exceptions of the crib quilt and wall hangings, all of the Weekend Star quilts are approximately 84 inches by 100 inches, or double/queen size. Most of the blocks finish to 20 inches square. Adding an extra horizontal row of blocks will make a king size quilt; dropping a vertical row of blocks will make a twin size quilt. Changing the number and/or width of the borders are easy ways to make slight adjustments in the size of your quilt. See Before Adding Borders, page 9.

In case you are wondering about the size, I use these quilt size guidelines. Except for the crib size, they were developed by adding 9 inches for a pillow tuck at one narrow end and a 13-inch drop to the other three sides of standard mattress sizes.

Crib-	Small 30 inches x 45 inches
	Large 40 inches x 60 inches
Twin-	65 inches x 97 inches
Double-	80 inches x 97 inches
Queen-	86 inches x 102 inches
King-	104 inches x 102 inches

Because so many beds are either a Queen or Double size, and there isn't a huge difference in the size, 84 inches by 100 inches is a safe compromise size.

Fabric Selection in General

Most quilters prefer 100% cotton fabrics. Any fabric can be used if you understand the consequences regarding washability, shrinkage and other characteristics. For most of these quilts, I would recommend 100% cotton.

Learn to stand back and look before you buy or cut the fabrics selected for a quilt. There is a tendency to select fabrics at no more than an arm's length, but we rarely look at the finished quilt from that distance. Instead, it is viewed from "across the room." The fabrics can look very different then.

FABRIC SELECTION FOR THE QUILT FRONT

Fabric selection in terms of print style and color is very important. It does much more to set the mood of the quilt than the quilt design. Study the pictures of these quilts (pages 33 to 36 and front and back covers) and others to see what appeals to you. Almost any fabric combinations you like can be transferred to other quilts.

1. Selection of a color combination can be very simple, such as the turkey red and navy blue wall hanging, page 35.

2. Selecting the relationship of light to dark fabrics to maintain the definition of the design block is sometimes more important than selecting specific fabrics or colors. This is especially true of scrap quilts; see the Scrap Ohio Star, page 34.

3. If you want to make a multi-colored quilt, the easiest way is to pick a multi-color fabric that you love and has the balance of colors you want. Then select fabrics to coordinate. This method is especially successful if you can use the determining fabric as a border. See the Banded Jewel-tone Ohio Star Quilt on front cover.

4. Some quilts require several different blocks, or even all different blocks, to get the desired result. See the Country Mini Wall Hanging on page 35.

5. The easiest fabric selection mistake to make is monotony from over matching. In most quilts, a variety in color, scale and density of print designs, and mood help to prevent monotony.

BACKING FABRIC SELECTION FOR QUILT-AS-YOU-SEW QUILTS

Quilt-As-You-Sew quilts demand a separate piece of backing fabric for each block or section. If you want to camouflage this "block by block" technique, cut all the backing pieces from the same small random print. However, if you don't mind calling attention to this so-called "non-traditional" technique, and I don't, consider using more than one fabric. By cutting the block backs from different fabrics, I make eye-catching quilt backs and use up leftover fabrics so I can buy new fabrics for quilt fronts! The Scrap Ohio Star even has pieced blocks for the back of the quilt; see page 43.

A less complicated approach is to use two different fabrics for the block backs, set together checkerboard style, with a third fabric for the border backings. This is the way the back was made on the Good Luck in Ohio Idaho Iowa Star Wall Hanging. The back of the Banded Jewel-Tone Ohio Star falls in between. Nearly every block has a different color-coordinated back. The blocks were positioned randomly, page 27.

How Much Fabric Do I Need?

The quilts shown do have estimated yardage requirements. All estimates used in this book are based on 45-inch width fabrics unless otherwise stated.

Just as there is no single fabric yardage requirement to make a dress, there is not one answer for how much fabric it takes to make a quilt. Here are some rules of thumb. The backing for a double/queen quilt with one seam down the middle, requires 6 1/2 yards. So, if you allow fabric for seams and some latitude in cutting, I estimate a total of 10 yards for the surface of a not too complicated dou-

3

ble/queen quilt. Following the same line of thought, a total of 12 1/2 yards for a king and 6 1/2 yards for a twin.

Quilt-As-You-Sew rarely requires more fabric for the quilt front than traditional methods. However, slightly larger quantities of backing fabric could be required because of the piecing and finishing strips.

Nearly everyone agrees having extra is better than agonizing about running out. More and more I find I use my extra yardage for pieced backs for quilts or in pillow cases. I put decorative pillow cases on top of the quilt propped against the head board, then I don't have to fight the pillow tuck battle.

The question about fabric was, "How much do I need?" I have found that what I need and what I want are two different things. My policy has always been to buy as much as I could afford. Once you start making lots of quilts, you have a real appreciation for sewing from a stockpile of fabric.

All measurements in this book are in inches and yards, please use this conversion chart for centimeters and meters.

> 1 meter = 39.37 inches, so yards x .9144 = meters
>
> 1 inch = 2.54 centimeters, so inches x 2.54 = centimeters

Fabric Preparation

TO SHRINK OR NOT?

Contrary to nearly every article or book you have read, prewashing your fabrics before use is not mandatory. My choice is to test my fabrics for shrinking and bleeding before using, but not to automatically prewash. I like the crispness of the fabric before it is washed; and it is easier to use in the machine piecing and quilting techniques that I favor.

To test fabrics, cut the same size strip (2 inches x 12 inches is a good size) of each fabric. Wet strips completely in hot water, squeeze and iron dry. It is heat on wet fiber that really causes the shrinkage. At the same time, look for any color bleeding. If any fabric bleeds or shrinks beyond the 2% to 3% allowed by industry standards, I prewash that fabric or select another fabric. This 2% to 3% translates as 3/4 inch to 1 inch in a yard or 1/4 inch to 1/3 inch in 12 inches. If one fabric shrinks considerably more than the others, it is a greater problem than if they all shrink the same little amount.

HOW TO PRESHRINK

If you do preshrink, I recommend the following procedures.

For small amounts of fabric (assorted scraps), the solution is simple. Simply run hot water over the fabric pieces until they are saturated, then iron them dry. This is perfect because it is the heat on the wet fibers that causes shrinkage.

For larger pieces of fabric, sort by similar colors and put fabrics in your washing machine. Use the dial to by-pass all steps except the last rinse and spin-dry cycles. Use cold water and no detergent; hot water is not necessary, and may promote color fading. (Although it is the heat on

wet fibers that causes shrinkage, the dryer will be adequate for the job.) Detergent also facilitates color fading.

Then dry the fabrics in your dryer, but don't over dry. Press each piece with a steam iron. If any fabric is unusually limp, spray it with sizing (not starch) when you press.

The fallacy in this method is that it doesn't give you an opportunity to look at individual fabrics for colorfastness. If you are not familiar with the fabrics, you can dip a corner of each one into warm water in a large, clear bowl. Squeeze out the water, looking for any telltale signs of bleeding. Lay aside questionable fabrics and retest. It may be necessary to wash these fabrics separately until there is no sign of bleeding or running color.

Batting Selection

WHAT KIND?

To me, the best batting for bed quilts made using Quilt-As-You-Sew techniques is a medium-weight bonded polyester batting. Batting that is very thin just won't puff enough for this method. If it's too thick, it is difficult to work with. Look for batting which is bonded throughout, not just on the surface. Surface bonded batting can separate when washed. Look for a bonded batt that is reasonably soft. Suitable varieties are Hobbs Polydown, Fairfield Light and many of the battings sold on a roll in fabric stores. Just make sure the roll batts aren't stiff. Machine quilting is stiffer than hand quilting and a stiff batt results in a quilt that is too stiff.

For wall quilts, I often use the new lightweight polyester battings (such as Thermore® by Hobbs) or one of the new cotton batts (such as Heirloom Cotton by Hobbs). These batts give a flatter look that I prefer for a wall quilt. In addition, I frequently add more machine quilting to the surface of a wall quilt. The more I plan to quilt, the flatter I like the batt. The main problem with cotton batting in Quilt-As-You-Sew quilts is its density at the seams. Although cotton batting is flatter than medium-weight polyester, it is also much heavier.

The new cotton batts are very different from the cotton batts in antique quilts. The old cottons needed to be quilted very closely to prevent balling up when washed; manufacturers claim the new batting can be more loosely quilted. Cotton was used in the Country Mini Wall Hanging, page 35.

WHAT SIZE BATTING?

As a rule of thumb for selecting packaged batting, choose the next size up from the size quilt you are making. When using the Quilt-As-You-Sew method, cutting a separate square of batting with seam allowances, for each block generally requires more batting than would be in the same size of packaged batting. The narrow width of most roll battings (usually 48 inches) is not a problem for Quilt-As-You-Sew quilts (it has to be cut into small pieces anyway).

PREPARING THE BATTING

Remove packaged batting from its bag a day or two ahead of time so it can relax. A careful steam press eliminates humps and bumps. Put a lightweight fabric over either polyester or cotton batting to protect it from the hot iron.

Smoothing the batting will make cutting the squares more accurate and Quilt-As-You-Sew easier.

CUTTING THE BATTING

It is very easy to cut batting with a rotary cutter, and the clean cut is nice to use. The problem is that the fibers from polyester batting seem to be forced into the mat by the blade. The result is a slightly furry mat. My solution is to use one of my old mats exclusively for cutting batting squares. If you don't have the luxury of an old mat, you may be able to use the second side of your mat for batting only.

When it's time to trim the sewn quilt blocks (Perfecting the Block Shape and Size, page 7), the layer of fabric between the batting and the board protects the cutting board.

Do not cut batting and backing strips for the borders yet. It is better to wait until the quilt interior is put together and you know the exact measurements than to use the approximate measurements in the text. However, you can eliminate a lot of piecing if you plan the border pieces and leave long strips of fabric and batting.

Tools

THE SEWING MACHINE

It goes without saying that your sewing machine is the most important tool for making a quilt in a weekend! If you haven't used it recently, dust it off, oil it and change the needle. You don't need a fancy machine. If the presser foot is pushing the layers out of alignment, you can usually correct that by reducing the pressure on the presser foot. (See your sewing machine manual for instructions.) If you have an even feed attachment, you may want to use it.

OTHER NECESSITIES

Set up a steam iron and ironing board next to your sewing machine.

Most other tools are probably already in your sewing supplies. A small ruler or hem gauge, kept handy for double-checking strip widths and seam allowances, is especially helpful for ensuring accuracy when piecing. You will also need good small scissors, a seam ripper, thimbles, hand sewing needles, etc. As you quilt more, you will probably want to add some specialized quilting tools like erasable fabric marking pens and pencils, smaller acrylic rulers and squares.

THE ROTARY CUTTER

Next to your sewing machine, a good cutting center is the most important tool for successful Quilt-As-You-Sew projects. Accurate cutting is crucial. The rotary cutter system has really revolutionized the ease of cutting most shapes. Some of my quilt-making friends love the quilting most, some the piecing process, but I don't know anyone who loves the cutting. Yet accurate cutting is the first crucial step to accurate patchwork. The rotary cutter looks like an advanced pizza cutter. It must be used in conjunction with a special protective mat and is most effective with a rigid, thick acrylic ruler for long smooth cuts!

There are many different acrylic rulers 5 inches or 6 inches wide and 24 inches long. They are usually printed with a grid on the ruler surface that is very helpful in assuring accuracy. Most rulers also have angles and other special printed features. With just a little practice, you'll be comfortable cutting nearly any straight line geometric shape with just a ruler and rotary cutter, further eliminating the need for patterns, templates, and tedious tracing. Refer to The Rotary Cutting Key, page 16, for information on converting pattern pieces to rotary cutting directions.

With the rotary cutting method, you can be faster than with scissors, but more importantly, you can be more accurate than with scissors. You can accomplish the cutting processes outlined in this book with a ruler, pencil and scissors, but you'll save time measuring, save time cutting, and be more accurate with the rotary cutter method. Some shapes must be cut with scissors, however, so don't throw them out altogether!

TIPS FOR USING THE ROTARY CUTTER

• The blades are very sharp. All of the brands currently available have guards. Make sure they are in place when the cutter is not in use. This protects both you and the blade. If you drop the cutter or accidentally cut across a pin, the blade often becomes nicked. Then instead of cutting the fabric where the blade is nicked, it perforates the fabric. The blades are replaceable, but the need can be minimized if you will just keep the guard in place.

• A fresh blade will cut 6 to 12 layers of fabric easily with very little pressure. Bearing down too hard is not necessary and can do irreparable damage to the protective mat. It's harder to accurately fold and stack 12 layers of fabric than to cut them. For that reason, I generally cut 4 to 8 layers even though the cutter could cut more.

• When cutting, the blade side, not the guard side, goes immediately next to the acrylic ruler.

• Cut away from you, not toward your body, **Fig A**.

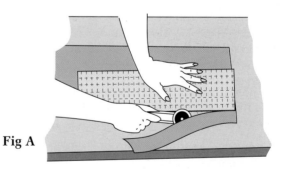

Fig A

• The first cut is usually trimming off the selvage (cutting strips on the lengthwise grain) or straightening a store cut edge (cutting strips on the crosswise grain). To make a strip, the next cut is the second side of the first strip. It requires changing hands, going to the other side of the mat, or turning the mat. My favorite method is to cut the first strip left-handed—not as hard as it sounds if you have a good ruler—and the rest right-handed, which is my favored hand; then I don't have to change table sides or turn the fabric or mat.

• Take advantage of the grids on the mat and on the ruler to maximize your accuracy. To get straight strips, it is imperative that the ruler be perpendicular to the fold on folded fabrics and/or parallel to the selvage.

• No matter what the final shape is to be, it is most common to first cut a strip that is the same width as one dimension of the desired piece, then cut across the strip to get the shape needed, **Fig B**.

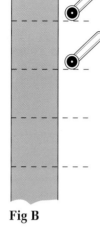

Fig B

Cutting the Fabrics for the Weekend Star Quilts

Some people may prefer to use templates and cut separate pieces for the Weekend Star blocks individually. Pattern pieces are included so you can do that. Rotary cutting is faster, easier, and almost always more accurate, and this book has innovative ways to incorporate these techniques into Weekend Star quilts. To do this most easily and efficiently, you need a rotary cutter system. (See earlier discussion.)

CUTTING ON THE LENGTHWISE GRAIN

Pattern pieces are marked with an arrow to designate alignment on the lengthwise grain, but what about strips when rotary cutting, or for borders and binding?

When working with strips, I prefer to cut strips on the lengthwise, not crosswise grain. Because many dress pattern pieces are marked "Place on the lengthwise or crosswise grain," there is a tendency to think there is no difference. Tug on the same piece of woven fabric in both directions and you'll see that the lengthwise grain is much firmer, **Fig C**. The crosswise grain can stretch 2 1/2 to 3 times farther than the lengthwise grain. Bias runs diagonally across the lengthwise and crosswise grains of the fabric, and is the most stretchy

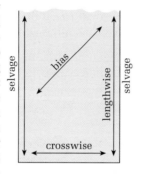

Fig C

direction of a piece of fabric. This is the main reason I stress lengthwise grain on the longest dimension of a piece whenever possible.

Another important reason for cutting strips on the lengthwise grain revolves around the fabric problem called "bowing," **Fig D**. That is the word used to describe the problem of threads being pulled out of position during the printing and finishing process. Crosswise threads, instead of being perfectly perpendicular to the selvage, are arched. If you then cut cross-

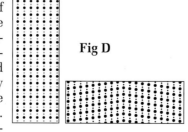

Fig D

wise strips, you are cutting (breaking) every crosswise thread you hit. Everywhere threads are cut, they will ravel. (Theoretically, if you were cutting crosswise strips, you would be cutting between two perfectly parallel crosswise threads and only cutting lengthwise threads.)

In addition when fabric is bowed, any directional design in the fabric is pulled out of position, too. Cutting crosswise strips makes that distortion more obvious, especially in a sashing strip on the outside edge of a Weekend Star block.

Bowing barely effects lengthwise grain. Cutting strips on the lengthwise grain keeps printed patterns more accurate and greatly reduces raveling.

There are two things that might cause me to cut on the crosswise grain. One, simple economics; that is I only need or have a little bit of a particular fabric. If you cut lengthwise strips from a quarter yard of fabric, you can hardly call it a strip. Two, the design demands of a directional fabric will always override grainline cutting rules.

Seams and Such

SEAM ALLOWANCES

The recommended seam allowance is 1/4 inch, using 10 - 12 stitches per inch. It is not necessary to backstitch the seams as you will stitch across most ends almost immediately. (It is, however, a good idea to keep threads clipped on both the front and the back so they don't get caught in subsequent seams.) If your machine has an automatic stitch-in-place or stitch tie-off, use it, but don't panic if you forget.

If you are new to patchwork, you may not have entered the world of the 1/4-inch seam allowance yet. After using 5/8-inch seam allowances in dressmaking, the first 1/4-inch seam will look impossibly thin. Remember, in dressmaking, many 5/8-inch seam allowances survive being trimmed smaller than 1/4 inch, turned inside out and poked. Not only is the 1/4-inch seam allowance adequate for patchwork, but if it is necessary to make a narrower seam allowance, don't worry until you get below 1/8 inch.

On many sewing machines the outside edge of the presser foot is exactly 1/4 inch from the center of the needle hole. An easy way to measure is to put a tape measure under your presser foot, **Fig E**. Put any inch mark at the needle. Put the presser foot down. If it's 1/4 inch wide, you're lucky. If it isn't, you'll have to find some other way to calculate the 1/4-inch seam, like a mark on the toe of the presser foot. Tape or other marks on the sewing machine will be covered by the quilt squares.

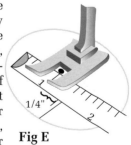

Fig E

THERE'S MORE TO PERFECT PATCHWORK THAN A 1/4-INCH SEAM ALLOWANCE

In the final analysis, it's the size of the piece between the seam allowances that is really important, not the size of the seam allowance. The seam allowance is there to keep the sewing threads from ripping out and to allow you to ake adjustments if necessary. The object is to have a perfect 1-inch square, for example, in the finished patchwork, ot to have a perfect 1/4-inch seam allowance. You can ver-emphasize sewing exactly 1/4 inch from the cut edge. 's fine when it works, and if you have both a perfect finshed piece and perfect seam allowance, you can feel very mug, but the most important thing is perfect size finished atchwork.

Ripping Tip
you must rip or "unsew," the gentlest way is best, especially hen you have sewn through batting, backing and two pieces of abric. On one side of the seam, cut approximately every sixth titch. A little experimentation will let you know if you can get by ith cutting every 7 or 8 stitches. Then turn the fabric over and ull the thread on the other side. When you cut at the right frequency, the thread just pops out as you pull. Go back to the first de and brush away the clipped threads.

Pressing

ressing is not an option. It is smart to make your iron one f your best friends as you embark on patchwork. My preference is a steam iron. When pressing regular patchwork eams (as in the pre-pieced sections of many of the quilts), oth seam allowances go in the same direction, not open s in dressmaking. Usually, the seams allowances are ressed toward the darker fabric. Time spent carefully ressing is time well-spent.

usually press first from the wrong side and then turn the rips over and press from the printed or right side of the abric. The object is to eliminate any tiny folds I might ave pressed into the seam. Tiny 1/32-inch folds don't eem like much until you multiply that times 2 for each eam and times 4 or 5 seams for a block and times 10 or 12 or the number of blocks.

Vorking with the Quilt-As-You-Sew method adds a new imension to pressing. Pressing blocks layered with batng and backing fabric requires a lighter touch so that the atting does not get flattened. Raise the iron slightly above he surface of the fabric, holding the iron at a slight angle o that its point presses along the seam, **Fig F**. Use steam.

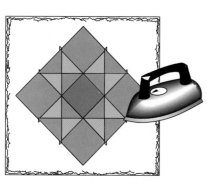

Fig F

Because polyester batting is more frequently exposed to high temperatures by the iron when using the Quilt-As-You-Sew method, guard against melting or damaging the batting (and the iron!) by using a press cloth or lowering the temperature of the iron. Melted batting aves residue on the surface of your iron which must be eaned.

Assembling the Quilt

These are the general assembly instructions. Specific measurements are included with each quilt shown.

Perfecting the Block Shape and Size

Before doing any assembly of blocks, trim them to a consistant size and shape. The shape for blocks in all quilts in this book is square. See specific quilt instructions for the exact size. In the Quilt-As-You-Sew technique, instructions are to cut the pieces of batting and backing larger than the mathematically correct finished size of a block. That means there should always be enough batting and backing. The perfecting process deals with size variations that may result from the actual piecing process.

Measure several blocks to determine the finished size of the design layer. It is easiest to do this with a large square acrylic measuring tool. After several blocks you will know whether you have a slight variance or huge. If the variance is large, you will need to carefully measure each one and sort by size. If there are only one or two very large or small blocks, you may prefer to make replacement blocks rather than compromise all the other blocks.

TOOLS FOR MEASURING

Ideally, we could have a piece of acrylic for every possible desired size of square and just lay it down and trim the edges with a rotary cutter. That, however, would require both a considerable cash expenditure and storage space. There are several large squares available, or two acrylic rulers can be used side by side. Determine what one half of the desired finished size should be and measure from the center of the block out to each side.

If you are working with a ruler and pen and scissors, make sure that you make right angles at the corners. Consider making a cardboard template to look through and use for marking a cutting line.

THE SUPER CUT!!

I have been making quilts using these techniques for over 15 years and only recently did I think of this wonderful step! For years I had accepted the fact that there would be some extra bulk where batting is sewn into seams. That's really no problem. However, where seams are sewn to seams at the quilt block corners, it can be just too bulky! So, there was always lots of trimming out extra layers of batting and seam allowances to reduce the bulk.

Thinking ahead is something I have always tried to do, but somehow I had never applied that process to this step. Why not trim before sewing? It works like a dream. Cut a small - about 3/8-inch square - piece of batting out of each corner of the batting layer, **Fig A**. Don't cut backing or design fabric, just the batting layer!

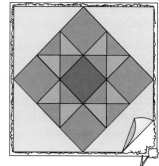

Fig A

Quilt-As-You-Sew Block Assembly

JOINING THE BLOCKS WITH FINISHING STRIPS

Perhaps you've been wondering how to sew the layered and quilted blocks together without having a lot of raw edges showing on the back. You're right, it can't just be a simple seam, there must be a way to cover the seam allowances. At one time, I used to work hard to disguise the "block by block" assembly method. It was quite laborious, and the part people didn't like. Now I make no attempt to disguise the method. Assembling the blocks with an added fabric strip to cover the seam allowance is my favorite way of finishing the blocks' raw edges.

1. Lay out the blocks in horizontal rows first.

2. The finishing strips are cut on the lengthwise grain 1 1/2 inches wide and about 1 1/2 inches longer than the length of the blocks to be joined. Press the strips in half lengthwise, wrong sides together.

3. Beginning with the first two adjacent blocks in Row 1, place right sides together with a folded strip on the blocks, aligning all raw edges. Make sure block centers match. Read Matching or Contrasting Finishing Strips, below, to determine on which block to place the strip. Pin the blocks and strip together, and stitch 1/4 inch from the raw edges through all eight layers, **Fig B**.

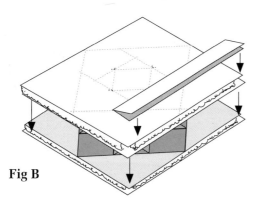

Fig B

4. Trim away the excess batting in the seam allowance. A friend discovered that if you pull the block firmly over your knee, the seam opens up and it is easy to trim away the excess batting between the layers of fabric. It is not necessary to cut away fabric, except at the ends of the blocks where the next seam will be.

5. After trimming the batting, press the strip to the side so that it covers the raw edges and hand stitch in place with a hidden stitch.

6. Join the blocks in each horizontal row in this manner. Read Alternating or Aligned Finishing Strips to determine which direction to face the strips from row to row.

Trim away any excess length of finishing strips after stitching in place, but before joining the rows together. See Joining the Rows with Finishing Strips, page 9.

MATCHING OR CONTRASTING FINISHING STRIPS

Sometimes, rather than try to camouflage the fact that I'm using finishing strips, I even make the strips decorative on

the back. If you have chosen a fabric for the finishing strip that contrasts with one or both of the backing squares, it important to decide on which square you wish the strip lie, and to take care to pin it to the opposite block befor stitching. The finishing strip is always pressed over th raw seam and stitched to the second block, **Fig C**.

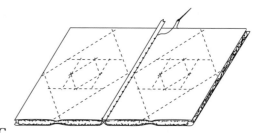

Fig C

ALTERNATING OR ALIGNED FINISHING STRIPS

Alternating strip direction in adjacent horizontal row reduces bulk at the seam intersection when the rows ar joined. Not alternating strips allows you to develop a gri system that lines up and creates a nice secondary patter on the back of your quilt, **Fig D**.

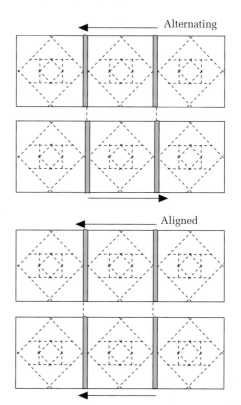

Fig D

Machine Hemming the Finishing Strips
*If you are clever with your sewing machine and know how to us your machine hemming feature, try hemming the finishing strip in that way, eliminating the hand stitching completely, **Fig E**.*

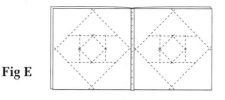

Fig E

JOINING THE BLOCKS WITHOUT FINISHING STRIPS

Sometimes there is not a machine stitch that goes all the way to the edge of the batting on one or more edges of the block. In that case, when two blocks are being sewn, it is possible to join the blocks without finishing strips. The only quilt in this book that is assembled by this method is the Good Luck in Ohio Idaho Iowa! Star Wall Hanging. Refer to page 51 for these directions.

JOINING THE ROWS WITH FINISHING STRIPS

Join the horizontal rows to each other with finishing strips. Cut strips on the lengthwise grain 1 1/2 inches wide by approximately 2 inches longer than the length of the rows to be joined. Line up the block seams carefully before adding the finishing strip. Proceed as for Joining the Blocks with Finishing Strips, above, considering to which side you wish the finishing strip to be hand stitched before pinning it to the rows of blocks to be joined. Trim away any excess length of finishing strips after hand stitching in place, but before adding borders or binding.

Adding Borders and Binding

Correcting Any Errors

Before doing any work with borders, it is important to measure your quilt carefully and accurately; make any adjustments needed. If you don't correct it now, any error just gets more exaggerated with each border.

Measure the length of the quilt from point to point, **Fig A**. If the opposite sides match, there are no errors to correct! Because you have trued up each of the squares before doing the final assembly and because of the stability of the quilted squares, the quilt sides will most likely match. If they don't match, now is your chance to correct them.

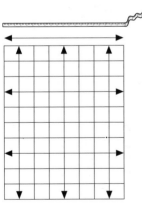

Always ease the longer side to make it the same length as the shorter side. The most important thing is that opposite borders are the exact same length.

Cut the borders the exact desired finished length plus seam allowances. Make the quilt fit the borders. If the quilt seems to be wrinkling, you may need to consider altering some of the quilt seams to correct the length.

Fig A

If You Must Piece the Border or Binding strips

*Cut the border strips on the lengthwise grain if possible. If you must piece the borders or binding, place the pieces at right angles and stitch diagonally as if you were piecing bias strips, **Fig B**. The seams are less visible in a border, and it eliminates bulk when the bindings are folded.*

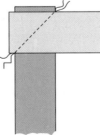

Fig B

Before Adding Borders

If you thought all your choices were over when the blocks were made, think again! Even though measurements are included for the borders on each quilt shown, the first step in adding borders to your quilt is deciding if the borders shown are really appropriate for the quilt you made. It is important that you feel free to design your own borders. The fabrics and set of each group of blocks strongly affect a quilt's look. The number and width of borders (and binding) that complement strong country colors may not flatter a pastel print version. Borders should be designed both to arrive at a certain finished quilt size, and to make the quilt as attractive as possible.

Adding Quilt-As-You-Sew Borders

Quilt-As-You-Sew quilt tops automatically require Quilt-As-You-Sew borders; therefore all borders for the quilts in this book have been added by this method. Quilt-As-You-Sew borders can be used on any quilt top that has been layered and quilted. (A modified method for use with traditionally pieced quilts is discussed on page 12.) As you make other quilts, you may want to adopt these techniques.

Standard Quilt-As-You-Sew borders are made with blunt ends (as opposed to mitered). The seam allowances of the quilt interior and the first border are encased, so that no finishing strips are required; any subsequent borders are added with the stitch and flip method. The batting and border backing strips should be as wide as the total width of all the front borders; therefore, they are cut much wider than any single border strip of a quilt with multiple borders. For quilts with a single border, the batting and border backing are cut only slightly wider.

If there is to be any additional surface quilting, it is most frequently done after the borders are added. That is the only method discussed in this book. **Weekend Basket Quilts** (ASN book #4146) does feature one quilt for which the border is quilted independently, and then added to the quilt.

PREPARING THE BORDER BACKING AND BATTING

Because all the quilts in this book are finished with a separate French-fold binding, the border backing and batting are cut about 1 1/2 inches wider than the finished width of all borders.

The step-by-step process below is illustrated using the Ohio Star quilt.

ADDING THE FIRST BORDER

1. Cut the border, batting, and border backing pieces needed for your quilt. Please note that in the individual quilt instructions, the cut lengths of borders are mathematically correct for the quilts as made; however, your quilt may be slightly different. Please measure your quilt before cutting your borders. All borders are cut the desired border width plus two seam allowances. Cut two side borders the exact length of the quilt top. The length of the top and bottom borders is the width of the quilt top plus twice the desired finished border width plus 1/2 inch for two seam allowances.

When cutting multiple borders for a quilt, always complete one round of borders before measuring and cutting the next fabric.

2. Add the side borders first. Lay the quilt on a large flat surface right side up, and put one of the side border pieces on top, right side down with one long edge lined up with the long edge of the quilt. Mark and match the center point and quarter points of both the quilt and the border. Pin in place sparingly.

3. To add the batting and border backing fabric, fold the edge of the quilt you are working on forward about 15 inches. Lay the backing fabric strip against the backing of the quilt, right sides together. Put the batting on top of it. Line up raw edges and ends then pin securely in place through all six layers, **Fig C**.

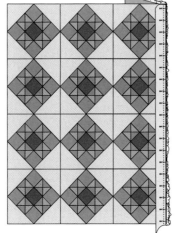

Fig C

4. Repeat steps two and three on the opposite long edge of the quilt.

5. Machine stitch 1/4 inch from the raw edges of both sides, through all six layers, the entire length of the quilt. Remove all pins.

6. Trim away any excess batting from the seams to reduce bulk, but do not trim closer than 1/8 inch or batting will tend to pull out of the seam. Pull the front border, batting, and border backing away from the quilt and bring them together so they are flat on the same surface as the quilt, **Fig D**. The batting is now sandwiched between the border and the border backing fabric. This is the one seam that I recommend pressing—preferably with steam.

Fig D

7. Position the top pieces of the first border, border backing, and batting as shown in **Fig E**. The strip of top border fabric does not go the full width of the quilt, as the batting and border backing do, but ends even with the outer edges of the side border strips. Trim the border ends to exact length as necessary. Pin securely, machine stitch, trim excess batting, and pull the borders forward, as in steps two through six. Press the seam. Repeat on bottom edge.

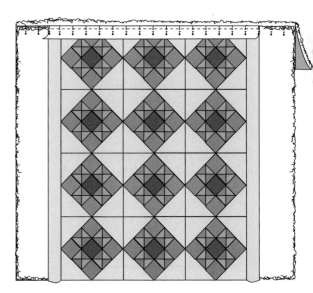

Fig E

ADDING SUBSEQUENT BORDERS

Now that the batting and border backings are in plac adding subsequent borders is quick and easy with t stitch and flip method. Always attach side borders fir and complete one set of borders before starting the next.

1. Pin the first borders flat. Along one long edge, place strip of the second border fabric on top of first bord right sides facing and raw edges matching; pin secure The ends of the second side border should line up wi the ends of the first end border, **Fig F**.

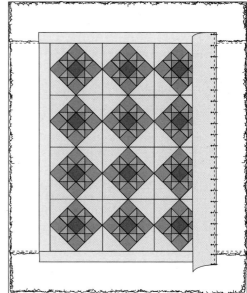

Fig F

2. Machine stitch through both borders, batting and ba ing fabric 1/4 inch from the raw edges of the borde Align and stitch the second long edge in the same man After removing the pins, pull the second border forwar lie flat on the batting. Press.

Add the second border at top and bottom of quilt. These strips go from one end of the second side border to the other, **Fig G**.

Repeat for remaining borders.

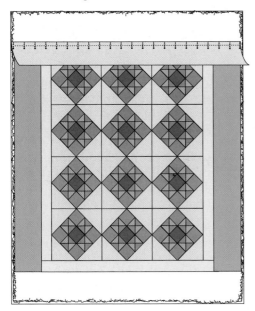

Fig G

ADDING A BORDER WITH CORNER BLOCKS

Cut two side borders the desired border width plus two seam allowances, and the exact length of the quilt. Add as above.

Cut the top and bottom borders 1/2 inch longer than the width of the quilt before borders. Cut four contrasting squares the same size as the cut width of the border.

Add one square to each end of the top and bottom border strips. Matching seams carefully, add borders as above, **Fig H**.

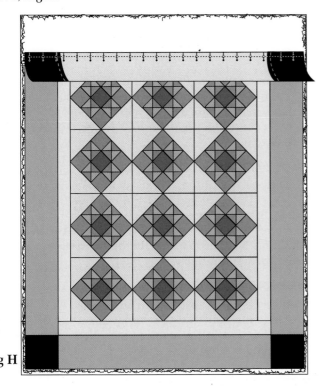

Fig H

ADDING A MITERED BORDER

The Banded Ohio Star, page 24, is the only quilt with mitered corners in the whole book. Even they are really mock mitered. There are several reasons. Mitered corners take more time, more fabric, more skill and lots more luck than blunt corners. When the same non-directional fabric is being used in the entire border, the resulting corners look the same whether they are blunt seamed or mitered, **Fig I**. In addition, I have a Theory.

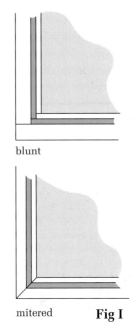

blunt

mitered **Fig I**

The Mitered Corner Quota Theory
I believe that we are all born with an unknown quota for the number of perfect mitered corners we can make in a lifetime. I would hate to be 85 years old and have a great floral striped border fabric that just had to be mitered and discover that I had used up my quota mitering something as undemanding as muslin. So I save my mitering for corners where it really counts.

There is a corollary to this theory that says, "Only three out of four mitered corners can be perfect on the same quilt on the first try!"

Borders that will be mitered have to be cut longer than blunt finish borders. When cutting blunt borders, the length of the top and bottom borders is calculated by adding the width of the quilt plus the width of two finished borders plus 1/2 inch. That is the way to calculate the length of all borders with mitered corners. They must be positioned perfectly and sewn to the side of the quilt stopping 1/4 inch from the end of the quilt. Press seam allowance toward quilt top.

To stitch a traditional miter, the quilt is folded at a 45 degree angle with the borders perfectly aligned on top of each other. Continue the fold line with the stitching, **Fig J**. This is much more complicated when border batting and backing are already attached to the quilt.

miter

fold

45°

Fig J

For a mock miter, work from the top of the quilt with one border extended flat and the other folded and pressed to make the perfect 45 degree angle. Pin in place and carefully stitch by hand with a hidden stitch, **Fig K**.

When corners are completed to satisfaction, trim away excess fabric and proceed. It is okay to miter one border, perhaps a demanding stripe, and not the others.

mock miter **Fig K**

Modified Quilt-As-You-Sew Borders

This method is used with traditionally pieced quilts; therefore, no quilts in this book are made with the Modified Quilt-As-You-Sew borders. However, because it is such a helpful machine quilting technique, and in case you decide to piece these quilts traditionally, it is described and illustrated.

Instead of adding borders to the quilt top and then layering and quilting the entire quilt, only the patchwork interior of the quilt is centered on the full size backing and batting (cut large enough to allow the total width of all the borders to be added). After that section is quilted, Quilt-As-You-Sew borders are added to the quilt. They are added just as they would have been by the traditional method, except that you will sew through the existing batting and backing at the same time. It is the same stitch and flip method used for Adding Subsequent Borders in the standard Quilt-As-You-Sew border. The point is, you have to make a seam to add the border fabric to the quilt top, so why not quilt at the same time?

1. Cut the batting and backing 2 inches bigger all around than the size of the quilt top plus the finished sizes of all the borders. Center the quilt top on top of the batting and backing, and quilt the interior. Measure and cut the quilt borders. Again, unless I have a fabric or design that demands mitering, I find crossed or blunt borders to be just fine.

2. After the quilt interior is quilted, lay it right side up on a large flat surface. Add the side borders first and then the ends, just as if you were adding borders before layering and quilting. When there are several borders, I prefer to add them one fabric at a time to create more quilting. Put the first side border right side down on top of the quilt as if you were making a regular seam, **Fig L**. Pin in place.

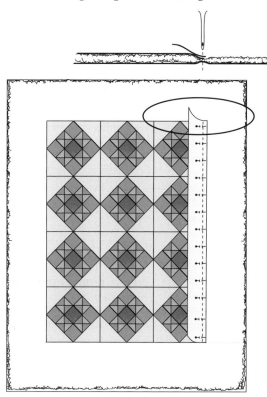

Fig L

Stitch through all thicknesses, quilting and sewing at t[he] same time. Repeat with the opposite side border. Op[en] new borders flat into the proper position before addi[ng] borders on the ends of the quilt. Pin or very lightly pre[ss] the first border flat before sewing across the end of it w[ith] another border.

French-fold Blunt Corner Binding

All through the book, I have stressed making decisio[ns] and considering different options. When it comes to bin[d]ing the edge of a quilt, however, the French-fold binding [is] the only method I intend to discuss. Also, I am very happ[y] with blunt corners on my bindings. If I were going to ent[er] quilts in competition, I would take the time to make o[ne] continuous binding with mitered corners. Not because [I] like it better, or the quilt is warmer, or because it mean[s I] love the recipient of the quilt more; only because I kno[w] most judges give more points for mitered-corner binding[s.]

Interestingly, even though I machine piece and machi[ne] quilt nearly everything, I still love a hand-finished bin[d]ing. That is, it is sewn onto the right side of the quilt [by] machine, wraps around the edge of the quilt and [is] stitched to the quilt back by hand.

A French-fold binding is double-folded and generally c[ut] on the straight grain. It is cut four times as wide as t[he] desired finished width plus 1/2 inch for two sea[m] allowances and 1/8 to 1/4 inch more to go around t[he] thickness of the quilt. The fatter the batt, the more yo[u] need to allow here.

WHAT WIDTH AND LENGTH?

My favorite finished binding width is whatever size [I] think looks best on that quilt. Some quilts need a subt[le] narrow binding and others look best with a large, hig[h] contrast binding. The most common, however, is abo[ut] 1/2 inch finished. With that width and an average full-si[ze] quilt, the equivalent of 5/8 yard of fabric is required f[or] bindings alone. Just like borders, I prefer to cut the bin[d]ing on the lengthwise grain (unless it is for a curved edge[)] and I avoid piecing bindings whenever possible.

To determine the length to cut the side binding strip, me[a]sure the quilt side. If you don't want to piece the bindin[g,] the strips need to be cut from fabric as long as the quilt. [If] you must piece the binding, do it diagonally as shown i[n] **Fig B**, page 9.

STABILIZING THE QUILT EDGE

Unless there is quilting very close to the edge of the quil[t,] it is a good idea to stabilize the quilt before adding th[e] binding. Machine baste a scant 1/4 inch from the raw edg[e] of the quilt top. Stitch through the top, the batting and th[e] backing on all four sides of the quilt. Excess batting an[d] backing will be trimmed away later.

ADDING THE BINDING

1. Fold the binding strip in half lengthwise with the wron[g] sides together and the raw edges even. Press. Bindin[g] strips are added in the same order as borders, sides firs[t] then top and bottom strips.

Lay the binding on the quilt so that both raw edges of binding match the raw edge of the quilt top, and machine stitch in place.

Now is the time to trim away excess backing and batting, but how much? To determine that, pull one section of binding flat, so it extends onto the excess batting. Because I like full feeling bindings, I trim the backing and batting to be almost as wide as the extended binding. In other words, the extended binding will be about 3/16 inch wider than the backing and batting when trimmed, **Fig M**. Assuming you started with a 2 5/8-inch wide binding strip, and measuring from the seam, not the edge of the binding, the batting and backing would be trimmed 7/8 inch from the seam line or 5/8 inch from the edge of the quilt.

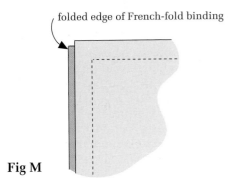

folded edge of French-fold binding

Fig M

Roll the binding around the raw edge of the quilt to the back, and hand stitch in place using the row of machine stitching as a stabilizer and a guide, **Fig N**.

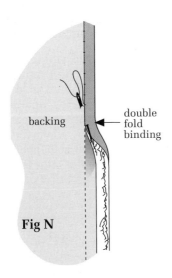

backing

double fold binding

Fig N

The hand hemming stitch I use is hidden. The needle comes out of the quilt, takes a bite of the binding and re-enters the quilt exactly behind the stitch. The thread is carried in the layers of quilt, not on the outside.

To make blunt corners (I feel mitered corners aren't necessary on most bindings), complete the hand stitching on the sides of the quilt before beginning the top and bottom bindings. Trim batting out of the last 1/2 inch of binding at the corner before completing the hand stitching. Trim away

in a staggered fashion other excess pieces of fabric so that the corners are not bulky and thicker than the rest of the binding.

6. Measure the quilt width carefully. Cut binding strips, adding 1/2 inch at each end. To eliminate raw edges, fold under the extra 1/2 inch at each end, before folding the strips in half lengthwise. Continue in the same manner as above.

7. Complete the hand stitching for the top and bottom of the quilt. At the corners, trim away enough batting and seam allowances to make the corners feel and look like the same thickness as the rest of the binding. Carefully stitch ends shut.

A MACHINE-HEMMED BINDING

If you are hemming the binding by machine, attach the binding to the quilt back and bring to the front. When you are stitching the binding to the front, you have the finished edge of the quilt as the positioning guide for the binding. It doesn't matter how much excess batting or backing there is. Remember, if you trim all of that away even with the quilt top, it is very likely that you will have a flat empty binding.

When you are stitching from the back, the only guide is the stabilizing stitch that you made that is a scant 1/4-inch from the quilt top edge. Either draw a line 1/4-inch outside that stitching or lay the binding so that it extends over the stitching.

Bring the binding to the front and either top stitch with invisible thread or experiment with your machine hemming stitch. The hemming stitch will take several straight stitches and then take a v-shaped stitch into the binding. On many machines there is a buttonhole stitch (on the Pfaff 1400 series, it is program #14) that can be used to create a tiny stitch I like to use for hemming, **Fig O**.

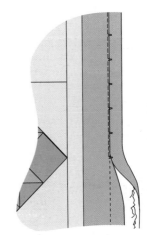

Fig O

TIP: Machine Hemming on a Pfaff
On the Pfaff, push the double needle position to overcome the computer set width of the buttonhole stitch and create a very tiny stitch. On programmable models, I have created my own stitch which I like better. It goes four stitches forward and then takes a tiny bite.

General Machine Quilting Techniques

In addition to Quilt-As-You-Sew techniques, other machine quilting techniques are also used throughout the book. This section includes a review of basic things I find helpful when machine quilting, as well as several techniques used in most or all of the quilts which are only referenced in the specific quilt instructions.

Nearly everyone wonders if they need a fancy machine to do the quilting. I have successfully machine quilted with all kinds of machines from very simple to the most expensive. Check your machine's quilting I.Q. on scraps first. If you have any problem, or don't like the look of the stitch, the first thing to check is the pressure of the presser foot. Too much pressure can make an undesirable rippling effect. Nearly every machine has an even feed attachment available that helps move all layers through the machine at the same rate. Some Pfaff machines have a built-in even feed, which, I must admit, is my favorite for machine quilting "in the ditch."

Machine Quilting "In the Ditch"

"In the ditch" refers to stitching in the space created between two pieces of fabric that are sewn together. "What space?" you ask. Granted there isn't much, so you create a little more space by applying a slight bit of tension on the seam line. Your fingers won't just walk, they'll pull away from the seam as the sewing machine feed dog pulls the fabric through the machine. That slight tension creates the extra space for stitching. When your fingers release the tension, the fabric returns to its natural position and tends to hide the stitching "in the ditch."

SETTING UP THE MACHINE

For most of the "in the ditch" quilting, I like to use invisible nylon thread for the top thread only. In the bobbin use a cotton or cotton-wrapped polyester thread that matches the color of the backing fabric. The invisible thread comes in both smoky and clear. I use smoky for everything but the lightest fabrics. The clear seems to reflect light and show more than the smoky. If I will be stitching on or beside only one color, I prefer to use the 100% cotton thread on the top also.

It is usually necessary to loosen the tension for the nylon thread. It is very stretchy and if the tension is too tight, the thread stretches while sewn and draws up and puckers when you stop sewing. I like a stitch length of 8 to 10 stitches per inch for quilting.

Free-Motion Machine Quilting

ADDS SURFACE QUILTING

The bonded polyester batting recommended for the Quilt-As-You-Sew technique should be adequately secured by virtue of the construction method. However, the current popularity of visible machine quilting and the ease of free-motion machine quilting may encourage you to add some additional quilting, especially in the borders.

ALLOWS QUILTING IN ANY DIRECTION

Straight-line quilting on the machine is really quite simple once you understand how to control the quilt and make it manageable. But what if you want to quilt in circles? Traditional sewing, where the feed dogs pull the fabric through the machine, would require somehow rotating the whole quilt around and through the machine. No way!

So what happens if you disengage or lower the feed dogs? Well, basically, the needle goes up and down, but the machine doesn't move the fabric, the feed dogs no longer control the direction that the fabric moves. That means you become the power moving the quilt under the needle, and you can move it any direction you want, even in circles. The good part is you don't have to pivot the quilt around the needle!

Free-motion quilting is done with the feed dogs down or covered and the regular presser foot removed. It is usually replaced with the embroidery or darning foot. When the presser foot lever is lowered, the darning foot doesn't actually touch the fabric, but it identifies where the needle will be stitching and is a safety buffer for your fingers. Even if you decide to stitch without a presser foot of any kind, the lever for the presser foot must be lowered as that is the same action that controls the tension on the upper thread.

PUTS YOU IN CONTROL

Free-motion means what it says. You can stitch any direction you want. Free-motion quilting allows you virtually complete control: you determine how fast the needle moves, and you move the fabric which direction and when you choose. The speed of the needle movement, and the direction and speed with which you move the fabric, determine the size and consistency of the stitch.

Practice first. Layer fabric with batting and backing, and hold the area where you are stitching taut. The easiest way to keep your stitch length consistent is to keep the fabric moving at a steady pace, and the needle moving fast. Remember though, that your stitch length will not have the same consistency as it does when the feed dogs and needle are completely synchronized. The hardest thing to believe is that the faster you sew, the easier it is to free motion quilt.

Begin by moving the fabric in any direction: write your name, make loops, just allow the stitches to develop.

The place where you are most likely to get puckers in machine quilting is where two lines of stitching cross. Now try to develop a random motion that goes forward, curves back and cuts back again without actually crossing a previous stitching line. This will create a nice quilted effect with little risk of puckers. With just a little practice you'll be amazed at the results.

When this random stitch that does not cross itself is done tightly or very close together, it is called stippling. Stippling is most commonly used to add interest to solid or near-solid colored fabrics.

If you plan to try fancy feather quilting on the machine, free-motion quilting would be the method to use.

Managing the Quilt and Yourself at the Machine

FOLDING THE QUILT

The trickiest part of machine quilting is fitting an enormous bulky quilt under the comparatively tiny arch of a sewing machine. The Quilt-As-You-Sew methods alleviate that because the major quilting in the interior is done in small easy-to-handle sections.

When you get to the borders, it still isn't necessary to work the entire quilt through the opening. The major width of the quilt is to the left of the needle. Make a 9- to 12-inch fold the length of the quilt. Fold again as many times as necessary to make a neat "package" to the left of the needle. Only the width of the border section needs to be dealt with to the right of the needle. If the border is wider than the opening, fold it down to the size of the opening.

Now you have a long narrow package. Either roll the quilt up, starting at the end opposite from where you will start sewing, or sit down and put the length of the quilt over your shoulder.

MACHINE AND BODY POSITION

If at all possible, I like to work with my machine set into a table so that it is not several inches higher than the table top. Whether that is possible or not, get your body high enough that your forearms can rest comfortably on the edge of the table. Sitting in an adjustable secretarial chair with the sewing machine at computer table height might be a suitable position. I have used a mid-height stool to raise the height of my torso but it still allows me to have my feet on the floor and a resting spot for my seat. The point is to avoid having to hold your arms up during this process, and to put your eyes in a position to see where you are stitching.

HAND POSITION

I see lots of people machine quilting with both hands on top of the fabric basically pushing their fabric around. This is fine for stitch-in-the-ditch quilting where the machine is pulling the fabric. It may even work for other people when they do free-motion quilting, and it may work for you, but it doesn't work for me!

My left hand is always under the layered fabric. Just grab from the back. It creates a slightly bunched area, but you don't hold in one place long enough to wrinkle.

My right hand rolls up and grabs the edge so that my hands are about six inches apart. Then I pull the fabric between my hands just enough to be taut. Most of the time, the fabric is actually raised off the surface of the machine so that the "drag" resulting from friction is reduced to a minimum.

This position is easier with blocks and border strips than is with full-size quilts, but I do it with quilts, too.

What About Thread?

Use invisible thread or cotton thread that matches the major color in the fabric. There is less tension hassle with cotton thread. Remember to loosen your upper tension with the nylon thread. Your actual stitches are much less visible with the nylon thread.

Weekend Quilts Without Quilt-As-You-Sew Blocks

Now that visible machine quilting is more readily accepted, nearly all of the quilts in this book could be made in a weekend by piecing the interior, layering and quilting that interior section, then adding borders following the Modified Quilt-As-You-Sew method on page 12.

The pattern pieces provided require no adjustments for piecing these quilt tops traditionally. If you don't choose the Quilt-As-You-Sew method, you may need to check some other sources for information on adding borders, traditional hand or machine quilting, and other finishing touches.

Traditional quilt backs are usually made from one fabric with minimal piecing. A single 45-inch width of fabric will do for many crib and wall quilts. Two pieces of 45-inch wide fabric pieced with a lengthwise center seam is the most common backing for a full-size quilt. For full-size non-Quilt-As-You-Sew quilts, buy wide roll batting or packaged batting to eliminate piecing the batting.

Terms to Know

In quiltmaking, it is especially helpful to make sure you know these geometric terms.

• **Diagonal** - Extending at a slant between opposite corners, **Fig A**.

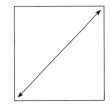

Fig A

• **Parallel** - lines extending in the same direction at the same distance apart so as to never meet, **Fig B**.

Fig B

• **Perpendicular** - a straight line at right angles to another straight line, **Fig C**.

Fig C

• **Right Angle -** a 90 degree angle; also called a square corner, **Fig D**.

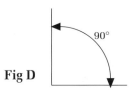

Fig D

• **Square -** a four sided figure having all of its sides equal length and all of its corners right angles, **Fig E**.

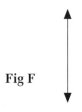

Fig E

• **Vertical -** straight up and down, **Fig F**.

Fig F

• **Horizontal -** parallel to the horizon; perpendicular to vertical; straight across, **Fig G**.

Fig G

Very Important

Even if you don't usually read introductions, please rea **this section about the pattern pieces and the exciting ne** **Rotary Cutting Key included in this book.**

About the Patterns

IDENTIFICATION

Most pattern pieces in this book are used for more tha one Weekend Star quilt. For this reason, patterns are ider tified by a continuous lettering system from the first quil to the last, rather than starting over with "a" for each quil Look near the Materials List of each quilt for the list of pat tern pieces required. Patterns appear on pages 53 to 61.

UNUSUAL SIZES

The cut size is included with each pattern for the rotar cutting key. You will see that these measurements are no always in simple 1/4-inch measurements. Don't panic One of the joys of the rotary cutting system is the availibil ity of accurate acrylic rulers with easy-to-follow grid lines It is even easy to measure sixteenths, if required: just lin the fabric up half-way between the eighths marks.

The Rotary Cutting Key

Although pattern pieces are provided, I prefer to us rotary cutter and strip cutting techniques for speed and accuracy. See The Rotary Cutter, page 5. To make thi even easier, each pattern piece features a key to rotary cut ting, which includes the cutting methods, the cut size and grain line markings.

Converting the Rotary Cutting Key to the *Metric System*
Measure the finished size with a metric ruler. Add an amoun *equal to two seam allowance widths that you prefer. My metric* *measuring friends tell me that there is not yet unanimity on th* *standard metric seam allowance. They say that even though 1/* *inch equals .6 cm, most quilters use either .5 cm or .75 cm for c* *seam allowance. Write the metric measurement, including you* *choice of seam allowance, into the book.*

CUTTING STRIPS

I prefer cutting strips on the lengthwise grain, see page 6 If I have 2 1/2 yards of a fabric, I don't want strips tha long, so I first cut a length of fabric no longer than 27 to 30 inches, and then cut strips on the lengthwise grain.

CUTTING SQUARES FROM STRIPS

1. In the rotary cutting key, there is a cut size for every pattern piece either inside the piece or right beside the piece. For squares, cut strips as wide as the cut size shown. That is, of course, the finished size plus 1/2 inch for two 1/4-inch seam allowances.

2. Then cut the strips into squares, **Fig A**. By definition that means you will cut across the strip with the acrylic ruler perpendicular to the previously cut edges. Make consecutive perpendicular cuts as far apart as the strip is wide.

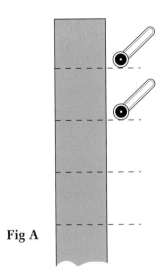

Fig A

CUTTING TRIANGLES FROM STRIPS

Triangles can be quickly rotary cut by cutting strips, then squares from the strips, then triangles from the squares. If you cut a square in half diagonally and make two triangles, **Fig B**, the hypotenuse is on the bias and the legs of the triangle are on straight grain. (That is assuming that the sides of the square were on straight grain.)

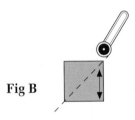

Fig B

If you cut that same square on both diagonals and made four triangles, **Fig C**, the hypotenuse is on the straight grain and the legs of the triangle are on the bias. Unfortunately, all three sides of a triangle cannot be cut on the straight grain! While it is best to avoid bias along the outside edge of a block, that doesn't always work.

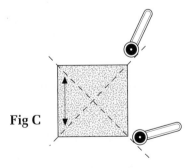

Fig C

Probably the best part of the rotary cutting key is that we have decided, based on the preferred grain for this piecing order, whether to cut two or four triangles from a square and what size square that needs to be for all of the triangles in the book. There are also grain lines marked on all triangle patterns in this book. However, the design demands of a directional fabric may override these decisions.

1. Cut strips the width indicated on the rotary cutting key.
2. Cut squares from these strips.
3. Cut the squares in half or quarters as shown on the rotary cutting key.

DETERMINING THE TOTAL NUMBER OF STRIPS NEEDED

To determine the minimum total strip length needed, multiply the total number of squares needed by the segment length for the second cut (for squares, the same as the strip width).

For triangles, if the rotary cutting guide shows two triangles from a square, divide the total number of triangles needed by two to determine the number of squares to cut. Likewise, if the rotary cutting guide shows four triangles from a square, divide the total number of triangles by four to determine the number of squares to cut. Then, the total strip length is determined, just as above, by multiplying the total number of squares needed by the square size.

GRAINLINE WHEN HANDLING TRIANGLES

Since there is no way to have all three sides of a triangle on the straight grain, we have to compromise.

The most important rule about bias is to handle it gently! Cutting triangles as marked on the patterns does not eliminate the problems that can come with bias. The grain lines marked on the patterns are appropriate for the pieced sub-units in the Quilt-As-You-Sew method of block assembly. Making the quilt top traditionally may necessitate adjustments.

USING A DIRECTIONAL FABRIC FOR TRIANGLES

One-way designs in fabric can add to the charm of a quilt, but extra fabric must be allowed, and extra care taken when cutting the fabric. See the photograph of the Banded Ohio Star Quilt on front cover. Because the fabric in this quilt has a directional print, half of the squares for **Pattern c** were cut diagonally from right to left, and half from left to right. To determine if directional cutting is necessary for your fabric, look at the design carefully before cutting triangles from squares.

Ohio Star Quilt

In reality, a quilt that is made in a weekend cannot be a showcase of tiny pieces, intricately assembled, and massively quilted. Instead, when time is a major consideration, the quilt design must incorporate the largest size pieces, and smallest number of pieces, possible, without going "over the line" to klunky.

This is the basic Weekend Ohio Star Quilt; all the remaining quilt instructions refer to this quilt. The mock diagonal set gives this Ohio Star quilt the appearance of a diagonal set without the work, **Fig A**. *Large corner triangles are added to the Ohio Star block, which is designed to be set on point. The new, larger block that is created is assembled using a straight set.*

Fig A

APPROXIMATE SIZE:
86 1/2 inches by 106 1/2 inches

BLOCK SIZE:
20 inches square

MATERIALS REQUIRED:
3/8 yd of navy print fabric
2 3/8 yds of ecru print fabric, including first border
1 5/8 yds of pink print fabric, including corner blocks for border and French-fold binding
3 3/8 yds of navy floral print fabric, including third border
2 3/8 yds of checked pink print fabric for second border
8 1/2 yds of backing fabric, including finishing strips
7 1/2 yds of batting

PATTERNS REQUIRED:
Use **Patterns a**, **b** and **c**, pages 53 to 61.

Tip: Make Any Block Suitable for Mock Diagonal Set
Make any 14-inch block, put it on point on a 21 1/2-inch square of batting and backing, add corners or corners with accent strips, and create a quilt block for a mock diagonal set quilt. This is even a good place for user-friendly fabric blocks (my name for printed patchwork).

Selecting the Fabric

One of the reasons for the popularity of the Ohio Star block is the way fabric choice can completely change the look of the block. Using dark or light, random or consistent, several variations are shown in **Fig B**.

Fig B

The easiest way to select the fabric is to pick a medium-sized multi-colored print. Select a neutral background for the Ohio Star and let the colors in the print guide you on the other parts of the block.

Shown in color on page 33.

The block diagram, **Fig C**, is shaded to represent the fabrics in the photographed quilt. The letters correspond to the pattern letters; number designations behind a letter can mean either a fabric variation or a grainline/cutting difference. Although directions are written for the photographed quilt, an empty exploded block with grainline indicators is included in **Fig C**, so that fabric substitutions can be made easily.

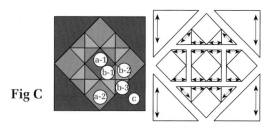

Fig C

Cutting the Fabric

For strip cutting techniques, refer to The Rotary Cutting Key with each pattern piece

1. From navy print fabric, use **Pattern a** to cut sixteen squares for position a-1.

2. From ecru print fabric, use **Pattern a** to cut forty-eight squares for position a-2. Use **Pattern b** to cut sixty-four triangles for position b-1. Use **Pattern b** to cut forty-eight triangles for position b-3.

3. From pink print fabric, use **Pattern b** to cut ninety-six triangles for position b-2.

4. From navy print fabric, cut forty-eight of **Pattern c** for the large corner triangles.

5. Cut twelve 21 1/2-inch squares of batting and backing fabric. Refer to Cutting the Batting, page 5. The finished size of the block is 20 inches; the blocks will be trimmed to 20 1/2 inches before they are joined.

Piecing Sub-unit #1

Before you begin piecing, study the directions and diagrams carefully. The order of assembly when piecing the Quilt-As-You-Sew Ohio Star block is quite different from the usual assembly, **Fig D**.

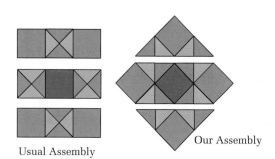

Usual Assembly

Our Assembly

Fig D

Make sixteen center square Sub-units #1 by sewing fo[ur] ecru print triangles to each navy square, **Fig E**, sewi[ng] opposite sides first. Finished sub-units should measure [ ] inches square, including 1/4-inch seam allowances.

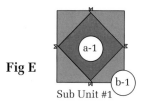

Fig E

Sub Unit #1

Set aside four of these sub-units to be used as corne[r] blocks in the second border.

Piecing Sub-unit #2

Make forty-eight Sub-units #2 by sewing two triangle[s] from pink print fabric to each ecru print square, **Fig [F]**. Twenty-four of these sub-units will be used as the base f[or] Sub-unit #3.

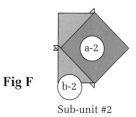

Fig F

Sub-unit #2

Piecing Sub-unit #3

Make twenty-four Sub-units #3 by sewing a triangle fro[m] ecru print fabric to each side of a Sub-unit #2, **Fig G**.

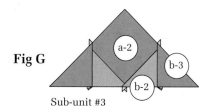

Fig G

Sub-unit #3

Assembling the Block

1. Layer the backing fabric, wrong side up, with the ba[t-]ting. Place Sub-unit #1 on top of the batting so that imag[i-]nary lines through the corners of center square are exactl[y] centered vertically and horizontally (10 3/4 inches fro[m] top, bottom, and sides), **Fig H**.

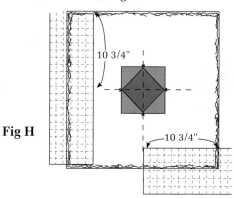

Fig H

10 3/4"

10 3/4"

Machine stitch "in the ditch" along the original seam lines, through the batting and backing (see page 14). Use monofilament nylon invisible thread in the top of your machine, and thread that matches the backing in the bobbin.

The "in the ditch" stitch can be done on all the remaining blocks at one time to reduce the number of times the thread is changed.

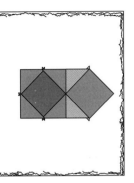

Step 1

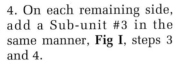

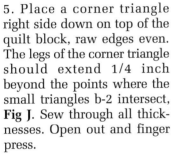

Step 2

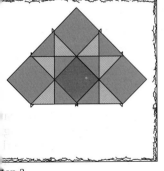

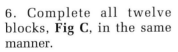

Step 3

3. Place one Sub-unit #2 on top of Sub-unit #1, right sides together and raw edges even. Seam lines should match. Sew through all thicknesses. Open out and finger press, **Fig I**, step 1.

Add another Sub-unit #2 to the opposite side of Sub-unit #1 in the same manner, **Fig I**, step 2.

4. On each remaining side, add a Sub-unit #3 in the same manner, **Fig I**, steps 3 and 4.

5. Place a corner triangle right side down on top of the quilt block, raw edges even. The legs of the corner triangle should extend 1/4 inch beyond the points where the small triangles b-2 intersect, **Fig J**. Sew through all thicknesses. Open out and finger press.

Finish the block with the remaining corner triangles, sewing opposite sides first.

6. Complete all twelve blocks, **Fig C**, in the same manner.

Joining the Blocks into Rows

1. Before joining the blocks, trim each block to 20 1/2 inches square, which includes 1/4-inch seam allowances. See Perfecting the Block Shape and Size, page 7.

2. Assemble the blocks into four horizontal rows of three blocks each. Finishing strips are used to join the blocks. From backing fabric, cut finishing strips on the lengthwise grain 1 1/2 inches wide by 22 inches long. For complete instructions, see Quilt-As-You-Sew Block Assembly, With Finishing Strips, page 8.

Joining the Rows

The horizontal rows are also joined together with finishing strips, page 8. Cut finishing strips 1 1/2 inches wide by 62 1/2 inches long.

When the quilt interior is completed, it should measure 60 1/2 inches by 80 1/2 inches, including 1/4-inch seam allowances.

Adding the Borders

The first quilt border is 1 1/2 inches wide finished, accented with corner blocks from pink print fabric. Cut 2-inch wide strips from ecru print fabric for the first border.

The second quilt border is 6 5/8 inches wide finished, accented with Sub-unit #1 corner blocks. Cut 7 1/8-inch wide strips from pink checked print fabric for the second border.

The final quilt border is 4 1/2 inches wide finished. Cut 5-inch wide strips from navy floral print fabric for the final border.

Please read Adding Borders and Binding, page 9, and Adding a Quilt-As-You-Sew Border with Corner Blocks, page 11. Also see the whole quilt diagram, **Fig A** on page 18.

Finishing the Quilt

A 5/8-inch French-fold binding finishes the quilt. Please refer to page 12 for details.

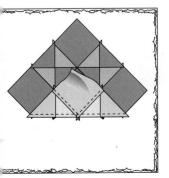

Step 4   **Fig I**

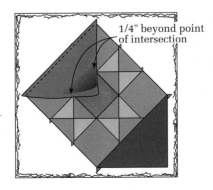

1/4" beyond point of intersection

Fig J

Variation-Octagon Ohio Star Block

A simple but very effective variation of the Ohio Star is the Octagon Ohio Star. This block is such a simple variation that we made only one block as a sample, shown in color on page 33, but there is a complete quilt layout, **Fig A**. This layout shows the same border plan as the basic Ohio Star, but could easily be finished with the borders shown next on the Banded Ohio Star. To make twelve blocks for the full size quilt, allow 7/8 yard of navy checked fabric for pattern d. All other yardage requirements are the same as for the Ohio Star quilt.

Fig A

APPROXIMATE SIZE:
Block Size: 20 inches square

MATERIALS REQUIRED:
All materials in Ohio Star list (page 18), plus 7/8 yd of navy checked fabric

PATTERNS REQUIRED:
Use **Patterns a**, **b**, **c** and **d**, pages 53 to 61.

The block diagram, **Fig B**, is shaded to represent the fabrics in the photographed block. The letters correspond the pattern letters; number designations behind a letter may mean either a fabric variation or a grainline/cutting difference. Although directions are written for the photographed quilt, an empty exploded block with grainline indicators is included in **Fig B**, so that fabric substitution can be made easily.

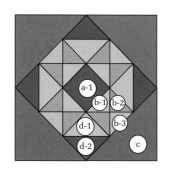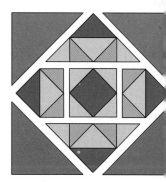

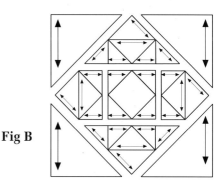

Fig B

Cutting the Fabric

For strip cutting techniques, refer to The Rotary Cutting Key with each pattern piece.

1. From navy print fabric, cut sixteen of **Pattern a**.

2. From ecru print fabric, use **Pattern b** to cut sixty-four triangles for position b-1. Use **Pattern b** to cut forty-eight triangles for position b-3. Use **Pattern d** to cut forty-eight triangles for position d-1.

3. From pink print fabric, use **Pattern b** to cut ninety-six triangles for position b-2.

4. From navy floral print fabric, cut forty-eight of **Pattern** for the large corner triangles.

Shown in color on page 33.

. From navy checked fabric, use **Pattern d** to cut forty-
ight triangles for position d-2.

. Cut twelve 21 1/2-inch squares of batting and backing
abric. Refer to Cutting the Batting, page 5. The finished
ize of the block is 20 inches; the blocks will be trimmed
o 20 1/2 inches before they are joined.

Piecing the Sub-units

The Octagon Ohio Star sub-units, **Fig B**, are assembled
ust like the basic Ohio Star block, except for step 2. Refer
o page 20 for more detailed directions.

. Make sixteen center square Sub-units #1 by sewing four
cru print triangles to each navy square, **Fig C**, sewing
pposite sides first. Finished sub-units should measure 7
nches square, including 1/4-inch seam allowances.

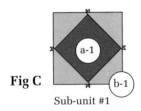

Fig C

Sub-unit #1

et aside four of these sub-units to be used as corner
blocks in the second border.

. Make forty-eight pieced squares by sewing ecru print
riangles and navy checked triangles together along the
ypotenuse, **Fig D**. Handle the bias edges with care.

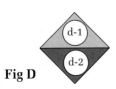

Fig D

. Make forty-eight Sub-units #2 by
ewing two triangles from pink print
abric to each pieced square, **Fig E**.
Twenty-four of these sub-units will be
ised as the base for Sub-unit #3.

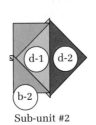

Sub-unit #2

Fig E

4. Make twenty-four Sub-units #3 by sewing a triangle
from ecru print fabric to each side of a Sub-unit #2, **Fig F**.

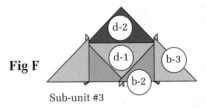

Fig F

Sub-unit #3

Assembling the Block

From here on, the Octagon Ohio Star block, **Fig B**, is
assembled just like the basic Ohio Star block. Refer to page
20 for detailed directions.

Completing the Quilt

Assemble the quilt top in the same manner as for the Ohio
Star. Use fabric requirements on page 18 and instructions
on page 21 to add borders and binding. However, you may
prefer the borders on the next quilt, The Banded Ohio
Star.

23

Banded Ohio Star Quilt

The Banded Ohio Star is another variation of the basic Ohio Star quilt. As in the basic Ohio Star, twelve identical Ohio Star blocks are set on point and corner triangles are added to create alternate blocks. The main difference is the addition of colorful bands of fabric between the Ohio Star block and the triangles. The bands accentuate the Ohio Star design while reducing the size of the corners for the mock diagonal set, **Fig A**. In addition, there is a considerable amount of meandering-style machine quilting, and a different border arrangement.

Fig A

APPROXIMATE SIZE:
80 inches by 100 inches

BLOCK SIZE:
20 inches square

MATERIALS REQUIRED:
2 1/2 yds of floral print fabric, including second border
1 1/2 yds of white-on-muslin fabric
3/4 yd of dark purple fabric
3/4 yd of dark teal fabric
5/8 yd each of medium purple, blue, magenta and medium teal fabric for contrasting bands and first border, cut crosswise and pieced
1 7/8 yds of stripe fabric for third border, cut crosswise and pieced
2 3/8 yds of border backing
twelve 21 1/2-inch squares of assorted backing fabrics, plus 5/8 yd for finishing strips, or 4 3/8 yds total of backing fabric
6 3/4 yds of batting
5/8 yd of fabric for French-fold binding

PATTERN REQUIRED
Use **Patterns a**, **b**, **e** and **f** on pages 53 to 61.

Selecting the Fabric

The block diagram, **Fig B**, is shaded to represent the fabrics in the photographed quilt. The letters correspond to the pattern letters; number designations behind a letter may mean either a fabric variation or a grainline/cutting difference. Although directions are written for the photographed quilt, an empty exploded block with grainline indicators is included in **Fig B**, so that fabric substitution can be made easily.

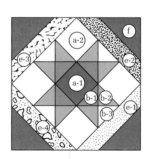

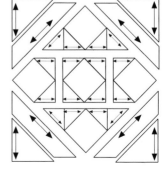

Fig B

Shown in color on front cover.

Cutting the Fabric

For strip cutting techniques, refer to The Rotary Cutting Key with each pattern piece.

1. From floral print fabric, use **Pattern a** to cut twelve squares for position a-1. Cut forty-eight of **Pattern f** for the large corner triangles. (Fabric in photographed quilt is directional; if you have also chosen directional fabric, refer to page 17.)

2. From white-on-muslin fabric, use **Pattern a** to cut forty-eight squares for position a-2. Use **Pattern b** to cut forty-eight triangles for position b-3.

3. From dark purple fabric, use **Pattern b** to cut forty-eight triangles for position b-1.

4. From dark teal fabric, use **Pattern b** to cut ninety-six triangles for position b-2.

5. From each of medium purple, blue, magenta and medium teal fabrics, cut twelve of **Pattern e** for the contrasting bands, positions e-1, e-2, e-3 and e-4.

6. Cut twelve 21 1/2-inch squares of batting and backing fabrics. Refer to Cutting the Batting, page 5. The finished size of the block is 20 inches; the blocks will be trimmed to 20 1/2 inches before they are joined.

Piecing the Sub-units

The Banded Ohio Star sub-units, **Fig B**, are pieced just like the basic Ohio Star block. Refer to page 20 for more detailed directions.

1. Make twelve center square Sub-units #1 by sewing four dark purple triangles to each floral square, **Fig C**, sewing opposite sides first. Finished sub-units should measure 7 inches square, including 1/4-inch seam allowances.

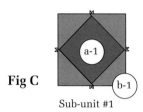

Fig C

Sub-unit #1

2. Make forty-eight Sub-units #2 by sewing two dark teal triangles to each muslin square, **Fig D**. Twenty-four of these sub-units will be used as the base for Sub-unit #3.

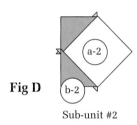

Fig D

Sub-unit #2

3. Make twenty-four Sub-units #3 by sewing two white-on-muslin triangles to each side of a Sub-unit #2, **Fig E**.

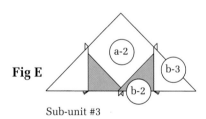

Fig E

Sub-unit #3

Assembling the Block

The Banded Ohio Star block, **Fig B**, is assembled just like the basic Ohio Star block until you reach step 4. Refer to page 20 for more detailed directions.

1. Layer the backing fabric, wrong side up, with the batting on top. Place Sub-unit #1 on top of the batting so that imaginary lines through corners of the center square are exactly centered vertically and horizontally (10 3/4 inches from top, bottom, and sides).

2. Machine stitch, preferably with monofilament nylon invisible thread, "in the ditch" along the original seam lines, through the batting and backing. Refer to page 14. Stitching can be done on all the remaining blocks at one time to reduce the number of times the thread is changed.

3. Continue assembling the block by adding sub-units opposite sides of the block, right sides together and r edges even. Match seam lines and look for clues that s units are properly aligned before sewing. Open out a finger press each sub-unit as it is added.

4. Now for the first variation. Sew contrasting bands to block in the same order as for sub-units, **Fig F**. If you ha chosen four different colors, make sure thay are in same position in every block.

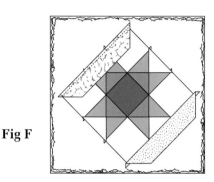

Fig F

5. To finish the block, stitch and flip the four corner tri gles in position, sewing opposite sides first, **Fig G**.

6. Complete all twelve blocks in the same manner.

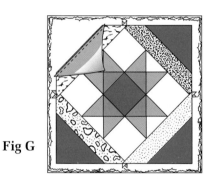

Fig G

Quilting the Blocks (Optional)

The white fabric selected for the background looked v empty. My choice was to add free-motion quilting in center square, and in the background squares and triang of each block, **Fig H**. There is no need to start and s when quilting, just move through the corners to the n section of the block as you quilt.

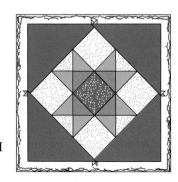

Fig H

Assembling the Quilt Top

1. Before joining the blocks, trim each block to 20 1/2 inches square, which includes 1/4-inch seam allowances. See Perfecting the Block Shape and Size, page 7.

2. Assemble the blocks into four horizontal rows of three blocks each. Finishing strips are used to join the blocks. From backing fabric, cut finishing strips on the lengthwise grain 1 1/2 inches wide by 22 inches long. For complete instructions, see Quilt-As-You-Sew Block Assembly, Joining the Blocks with Finishing Strips, page 8.

3. The horizontal rows are also joined together with finishing strips, page 8. Cut finishing strips 1 1/2 inches wide by 62 1/2 inches long.

When the quilt interior is completed, it should measure 60 1/2 inches by 80 1/2 inches, including 1/4-inch seam allowances.

Adding the Borders

The first quilt border is 1 1/2 inches wide finished, with mock mitered corners. Cut 2-inch wide strips from medium purple, blue, magenta and medium teal fabrics for the first border.

The second quilt border is 2 1/2 inches wide finished, with mock mitered corners. Cut 3-inch wide strips from floral print fabric for the second border.

The final quilt border is 5 1/2 inches wide finished, with mock mitered corners. Cut 6-inch wide strips from striped fabric for the final border.

Please read Adding Borders and Binding, page 9, and Adding a Mitered Border, page 11. Also see the whole quilt diagram, **Fig A,** on page 24.

Finishing the Quilt

A 5/8-inch French-fold binding finishes the quilt. Please refer to page 12 for details.

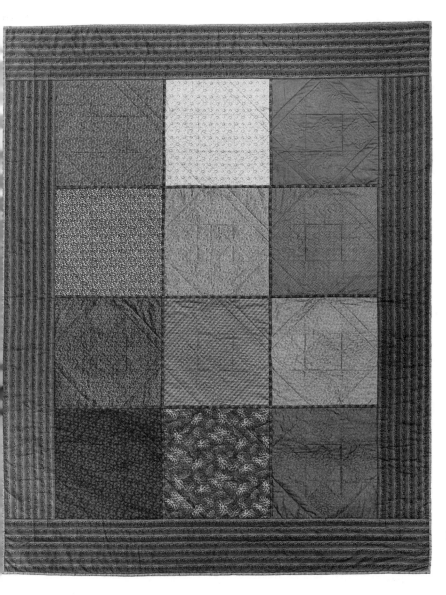

Back of Banded Ohio Star Quilt

Variation- Georgetown Star Quilt

APPROXIMATE SIZE:
Block Size: 20 inches square

MATERIALS REQUIRED:
All materials in the Banded Ohio Star list plus
1/2 yd additional floral print fabric
1/2 yd additional white-on-muslin fabric

PATTERNS REQUIRED:
Use **Patterns e**, **f**, **g**, **h**, **i**, **j** and **k**, pages 53 to 61.

An interesting variation of the Ohio Star block is the Georgetown Star. Once again, only one square is shown in color on back cover, but the Banded Ohio Star layout would be perfect for this quilt and is shown in **Fig A**. *To make 12 blocks for the full size quilt, allow approximately 1/2 yard more each of white-on-muslin and floral print fabrics than required for the Banded Ohio Star quilt; all other yardage requirements are the same.*

The block diagram, **Fig B** is shaded to represent the fabri in the photographed quilt. The letters correspond to t pattern letters; number designations behind a letter m mean either a fabric variation or a grainline/cutting diff ence. Although directions are written for the ph tographed Ohio Star quilt, an empty exploded block w grainline indicators is included in **Fig B**, so that fabi substitutions can be made easily.

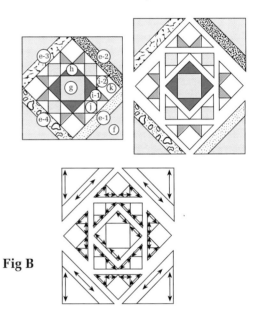

Fig B

Fig A

Cutting the Fabric

For strip cutting techniques, refer to The Rotary Cutti Key with each pattern piece.

1. From floral print fabric, cut twelve of **Pattern g**. C forty-eight of pattern j. Cut forty-eight of **Pattern f** for t large corner triangles. (Fabric in photographed quilt directional; if you have also chosen directional fabri refer to page 17.)

2. From dark purple fabric, cut forty-eight of **Pattern h**.

3. From white on muslin fabric, use **Pattern i** to cut 1 triangles for position i-1. Cut forty-eight of **Pattern k**.

4. From dark teal fabric, use **Pattern i** to cut ninety-six t angles for position i-2.

5. From each of medium purple, blue, magenta and me um teal fabrics, cut twelve of **Pattern e** for the contrasti bands, positions e-1, e-2, e-3 and e-4.

Cut twelve 21 1/2-inch squares of batting and backing fabrics. Refer to Cutting the Batting, page 5. The finished size of the block is 20 inches; the blocks will be trimmed to 20 1/2 inches before they are joined.

Piecing the Sub-units

Make twelve center square Sub-units #1 by sewing four dark purple triangles to each large floral square, sewing opposite sides first, **Fig C**. Finished sub-units should measure 7 1/2 inches square, including 1/4-inch seam allowances.

Make forty-eight Sub-units #2 by sewing two white-on-muslin triangles to each small floral square, **Fig D**.

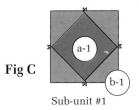

Fig C

Sub-unit #1

Sub-unit #2

Fig D

Sew dark teal and white-on-muslin triangles together to make ninety-six pairs of triangles, **Fig E**. Make forty-eight pairs with the teal triangle on the right side, and forty-eight with the teal triangle on the left.

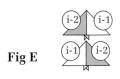

Fig E

4. Make forty-eight Sub-units #3 by sewing two triangle pairs to adjacent sides of a white-on-muslin square, **Fig F**. Be certain that the teal triangles are sewn adjacent to the square.

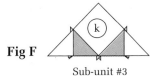

Fig F

Sub-unit #3

Assembling the Block

From here on, the Georgetown Star block is assembled just like the Banded Ohio Star block, **Fig B**. Refer to page 26 for detailed directions.

Completing the Quilt

Assemble the quilt top in the same manner as for the Banded Ohio Star. Use fabric requirements on page 24 and instructions on page 27 to add borders and binding.

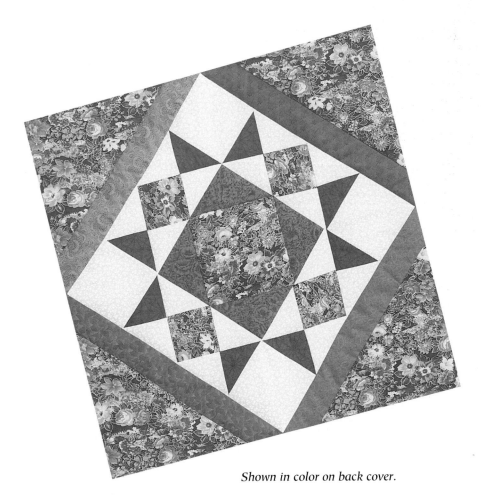

Shown in color on back cover.

Ohio Star Crib Quilt

*Isn't it true that we almost always have several month's warning on the need for a baby quilt? Yet isn't it common to wait until the last minute or even until after the birth to make, or even start, the quilt? Weekend quilts to the rescue! The Ohio Star Crib Quilt uses the same techinque as the Basic Ohio Star, just smaller pieces, **Fig A**.*

Fig A

APPROXIMATE SIZE:
43 inches by 54 inches

BLOCK SIZE:
10 3/4 inches square

MATERIALS REQUIRED:
1/4 yd of green print fabric
1 5/8 yds of ecru and pink print fabric, including first border and French-fold binding
7/8 yd of blue floral fabric
1 3/8 yds of pink print fabric, including second border
2 1/2 yds of backing fabric, including finishing strips
2 3/8 yds of batting

PATTERNS REQUIRED:
Use **Patterns j**, **m** and **n**, pages 53 to 61.

Selecting the Fabric

The blue print fabric set the color combination for thi unisex crib quilt. Each of the other colors was picked t coordinate with that print. Although two (very similar pink print fabrics were used in the photographed quilt yardage requirements are written as though you are usin the same fabric for the quilt block triangles, and the bor der. If you prefer to use a different fabric, you will need t purchase an additional 3/8 yard of fabric for the triangles.

The block diagram, **Fig B**, is shaded to represent the fab rics in the photographed quilt. The letters correspond t the pattern letters; number designations behind a lette may mean either a fabric variation or a grainline/cuttin difference. Although directions are written for the pho tographed quilt, an empty exploded block with grainlin indicators is included in **Fig B**, so that fabric substitution can be made easily.

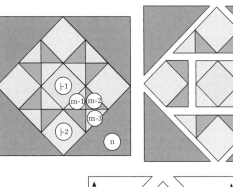

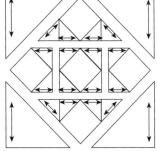

Fig B

Cutting the Fabric

For strip cutting techniques, refer to The Rotary Cuttin Key with each pattern.

1. From green print fabric, use **Pattern j** to cut sixtee squares for position j-1.

2. From ecru and pink print fabric, use **Pattern j** to cu forty-eight squares for position j-2. Use **Pattern m** to cu sixty-four triangles for position m-1. Use **Pattern m** to cu forty-eight triangles for position m-3.

3. From pink print fabric, use **Pattern m** to cut ninety-si triangles for position m-2.

4. From blue floral fabric, cut forty-eight of **Pattern n** fo the large corner triangles.

5. Cut twelve 13-inch squares of batting and backing fa ric. Refer to Cutting the Batting, page 5. The finished siz of the block is 10 3/4 inches; the blocks will be trimme to 11 1/4 inches before they are joined.

Shown in color on back cover.

Piecing the Sub-units

The Ohio Star Crib Quilt sub-units, **Fig B**, are pieced just like the basic Ohio Star block. Refer to page 20 for more detailed directions.

Make sixteen center square Sub-units #1 by sewing four ecru and pink triangles to each green square, **Fig C**, sewing opposite sides first. Finished sub-units should measure 4 1/4 inches square, including 1/4-inch seam allowances.

Set aside four of these sub-units to use as corner blocks in the second border.

2. Make forty-eight Sub-units #2 by sewing two pink triangles to each ecru and pink square, **Fig D**. Twenty-four of these sub-units will be used as the base for Sub-unit #3.

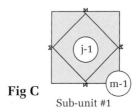

Fig C

Sub-unit #1

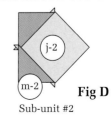

Fig D

Sub-unit #2

3. Make twenty-four Sub-units #3 by sewing a triangle from ecru and pink fabric to each side of a Sub-unit #2, **Fig E**.

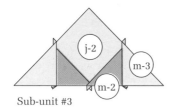

Fig E   Sub-unit #3

Assembling the Block

The Ohio Star Crib Quilt block, **Fig B** (page 30), is assembled just like the basic Ohio Star block. Refer to page 20 for more detailed directions.

1. Layer the backing fabric, wrong side up, with the batting on top. Place Sub-unit #1 on top of the batting so that imaginary diagonal lines through the center square are exactly centered vertically and horizontally (6 1/2 inches from top, bottom, and sides).

2. Machine stitch "in the ditch" along the original seam lines, through the batting and backing. Refer to page 14. Stitching can be done on all the remaining blocks at one time to reduce the number of times the thread is changed.

3. Continue assembling the block by adding sub-units to opposite sides of the block, right sides together and raw edges even. Match seam lines and look for clues that sub-units are properly aligned before sewing. Open out and finger press each sub-unit as it is added.

4. Finish the block with the four corner triangles, sewing opposite sides first.

5. Complete all twelve blocks in the same manner.

Assembling the Quilt Top

1. Before joining the blocks, trim each block to 11 1/ inches square, which includes 1/4-inch seam allowance See Perfecting the Block Shape and Size, page 7.

2. Assemble the blocks into four horizontal rows of thre blocks each. Finishing strips are used to join the block From backing fabric, cut finishing strips on the lengthwi grain 1 1/2 inches wide by 13 inches long. For comple instructions, see Quilt-As-You-Sew Block Assembly, Wit Finishing Strips, page 8.

3. The horizontal rows are also joined together with finish ing strips, page 8. Cut finishing strips 1 1/2 inches wide b 35 1/2 inches long.

When the quilt interior is completed, it should measure 3 3/4 inches by 43 1/2 inches, including 1/4-inch sea allowances.

Adding the Borders

The first quilt border is 1 inch wide finished, accente with corner blocks from green print fabric. Cut 1 1/2-inc wide strips from ecru and pink print fabric for the fir border.

The second quilt border is 3 7/8 inches wide finishe accented with Sub-unit #1 corner blocks. Cut 4 3/8-inc wide strips from pink print fabric for the second border.

Please read Adding Borders and Binding, page 9, an Adding a Quilt-As-You-Sew Border with Corner Block page 11. Also see the diagram of the completed crib qui **Fig A** on page 30.

Finishing the Quilt

A 1/2-inch French-fold binding finishes the quilt. Plea refer to page 12 for details.

Octagon Ohio Star Block

Country Mini Wall Hanging

Ohio Star Wall Hanging

Good Luck Star Block

Ohio Star Wall Hanging

This quilt is made with the same size block as the crib quilt. See what a different look can be created by changing the fabric and making three less blocks for a square quilt, Fig A.

Fig A

APPROXIMATE SIZE:
43 inches by 43 inches

BLOCK SIZE:
10 3/4 inches square

MATERIALS REQUIRED:
3/8 yd of red print fabric
3/4 yd of ecru print fabric
3/8 yd of small navy print fabric
5/8 yd of red checked fabric
1 yd of small ecru print fabric for border and French-fold binding
5/8 yd of navy print fabric for border
2 1/4 yds of backing fabric, including finishing strips
2 1/8 yds of batting

PATTERNS REQUIRED:
Use **Patterns j**, **m** and **n**, pages 53 to 61.

Selecting the Fabric

Most of the quilts in this book have a multi-color print that establishes the color scheme. This quilt, however, is simply, the ever-popular red, white and blue combination in its antiqued shades. The same effect could be created with any two colors you like together and an appropriate neutral background.

The block diagram, **Fig B**, is shaded to represent the fabrics in the photographed quilt. The letters correspond to the pattern letters; number designations behind a letter may mean either a fabric variation or a grainline/cutting difference. Although directions are written for the photographed quilt, an empty exploded block with grainline indicators is included in **Fig B**, so that fabric substitutions can be made easily.

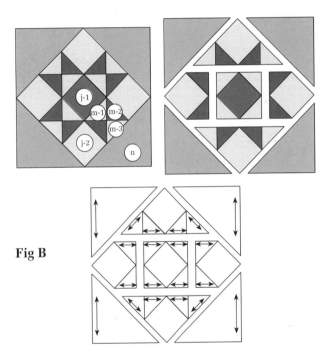

Fig B

Cutting the Fabric

For strip cutting techniques, refer to The Rotary Cutting Key with each pattern piece.

1. From red print fabric, use **Pattern j** to cut thirteen squares for position j-1.

2. From ecru print fabric, use **Pattern j** to cut thirty-six squares for position j-2. Use **Pattern m** to cut fifty-two triangles for position m-1. Use **Pattern m** to cut thirty-six triangles for position m-3.

3. From navy print fabric, use **Pattern m** to cut seventy-two triangles for position m-2.

4. From red checked fabric, cut thirty-six of **Pattern n** for the large corner triangles.

5. Cut nine 13-inch squares of batting and backing fabric. Refer to Cutting the Batting, page 5. The finished size of the block is 10 3/4 inches; the blocks will be trimmed to 11 1/4 inches before they are joined.

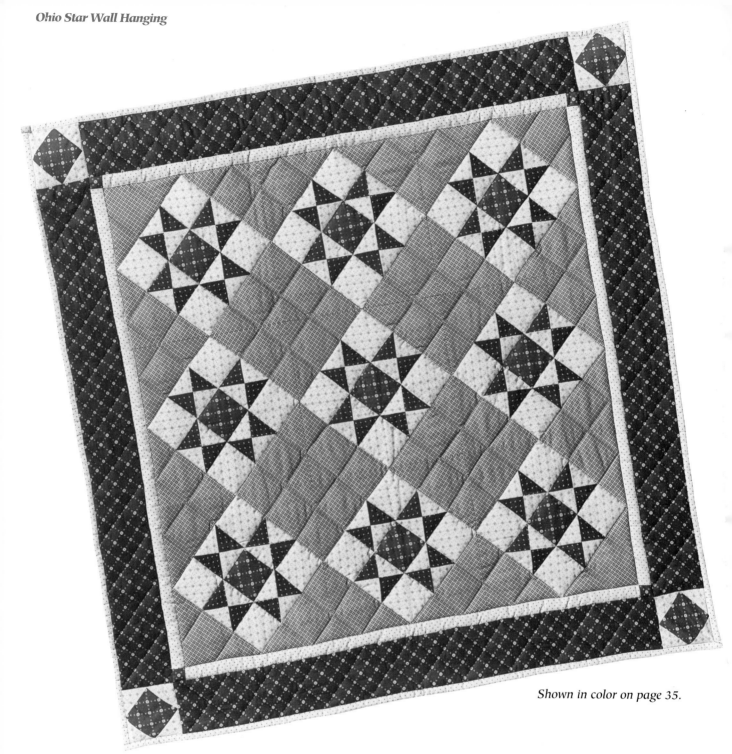

Shown in color on page 35.

Set aside four of these sub-units to be used as corner blocks in the second border.

2. Make thirty-six Sub-units #2 by sewing two small navy print triangles to each ecru square, **Fig D**. Eighteen of these sub-units will be used as the base for Sub-unit #3.

Piecing the Sub-units

The Ohio Star Wall Hanging sub-units, **Fig B** on page 37, are pieced just like the basic Ohio Star block. Refer to page 20 for more detailed directions.

1. Make thirteen center square Sub-units #1 by sewing four ecru triangles to each red square, **Fig C**, sewing opposite sides first. Finished sub-units should measure 4 1/4 inches square, including 1/4-inch seam allowances.

Sub-unit #1

Fig C

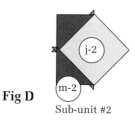

Fig D

Sub-unit #2

Make eighteen Sub-units #3 by sewing a triangle from u fabric to each side of a Sub-unit #2, **Fig E**.

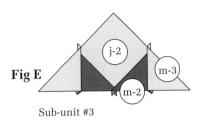

Fig E

Sub-unit #3

ssembling the Block

e Ohio Star Wall Hanging block, **Fig B** on page 37, is sembled just like the basic Ohio Star block. Refer to ge 20 for more detailed directions.

Layer the backing fabric, wrong side up, with the bat- g. Place Sub-unit #1 on top of the batting so that imagi- ry diagonal lines through the center square are exactly ntered vertically and horizontally (6 1/2 inches from p, bottom, and sides).

Machine stitch "in the ditch" along the original seam es, through the batting and backing. Refer to page 14. itching can be done on all the remaining blocks at one ne to reduce the number of times the thread is changed.

Continue assembling the block by adding sub-units to posite sides of the block, right sides together and raw ges even. Match seam lines and look for clues that sub- its are properly aligned before sewing. Open out and ger press each sub-unit as it is added.

Finish the block with the four corner triangles, sewing posite sides first.

Complete all nine blocks in the same manner.

Assembling the Quilt Top

1. Before joining the blocks, trim each block to 11 1/4 inches square, which includes 1/4-inch seam allowances. See Perfecting the Block Shape and Size, page 7.

2. Assemble the blocks into three horizontal rows of three blocks each. Finishing strips are used to join the blocks. From backing fabric, cut finishing strips on the length- wise grain 1 1/2 inches wide by 13 inches long. For com- plete instructions, see Quilt-As-You-Sew Block Assembly, With Finishing Strips, page 8.

3. The horizontal rows are also joined together with fin- ishing strips, page 8. Cut finishing strips 1 1/2 inches wide by 35 1/2 inches long.

When the quilt interior is completed, it should measure 32 3/4 inches square, including 1/4-inch seam allowances.

Adding the Borders

The first quilt border is 1 inch wide finished, accented with corner blocks from red print fabric. Cut 1 1/2-inch wide strips from ecru print fabric for the first border.

The second quilt border is 4 inches wide finished, accent- ed with Sub-unit #1 corner blocks. Cut 4 1/2-inch wide strips from navy print fabric for the second border.

Please read Adding Quilt-As-You-Sew Borders, page 9, and Adding a Quilt-As-You-Sew Border with Corner Blocks, page 11. Also see the diagram of the completed wall hanging, **Fig A** on page 37

Finishing the Quilt

A 1/2-inch French-fold binding finishes the quilt. Please refer to page 12 for details.

Scrap Ohio Star Quilt

This is the same size Ohio Star block as the previous two quilts. Obviously it will take lots of small squares to make a full size quilt—35 to be exact. This clearly is not a one-weekend quilt unless you have lots of helpers, but if you love scrap quilts as much as I do, it's worth the effort. When I'm going through this many different fabrics to cut pieces for a quilt, I like to cut pieces for at least one more scrap quilt at the same time—at the very least, I cut some strips for a Log Cabin or a scrap Nine Patch quilt. Since you actually cut from at least 70 different fabrics, cutting pieces for more than one quilt makes that much fabric handling seem more justified.

APPROXIMATE SIZE:
80 inches by 101 1/2 inches

BLOCK SIZE:
10 3/4 inches square

MATERIALS REQUIRED:
3/8 yd of dark print fabric (j-1)
5/8 yd of light print fabric (m-1)
35 assorted light print scraps, at least 8 inches by 9 inches (j-2, m-3)
35 assorted medium to dark print scraps, equivalent to approximately 12 yds (m-2, n and backing fabric)
1/2 yd of light beige print fabric for first border, cut cross wise and pieced
3/4 yd of medium rose print fabric for second border
7/8 yd of dark rose print fabric for third border
1 1/8 yds of dark green print fabric for fourth border
7 1/2 yds of batting
5/8 yd of fabric for French-fold binding

PATTERNS REQUIRED:
Use **Patterns j**, **m** and **n**, pages 53 to 61.

Selecting the Fabric
There are two common fabrics in every block of this scrap Ohio Star quilt. They are the floral center square (j-1) and the light background print that surrounds the square (m-1). These two were selected first. The remaining fabrics were chosen at random from assorted light, medium and dark scraps. The criteria for selecting these fabrics was, "A fabric can be used if it isn't UGLY with the original two fabrics." The fabric combinations may not necessarily be pretty, but we chose to use all combinations that were not awful! This manner of selection is very important to

achieving a random scrap look, **Fig A**. The star point (m-2), and the large corner triangles (n) are either medium or dark; the same fabrics were used to cut backing squar for the scrap back, too. The fabrics surrounding the sta (j-2, m-3) are all light.

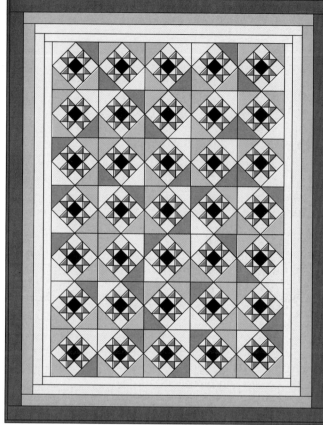

Fig A

The block diagram, **Fig B**, has letters which correspond t the pattern letters; number designations behind a lette may mean either a fabric variation or a grainline/cuttin difference. An empty exploded block with grainline ind cators is included so that fabric substitutions can be mad easily.

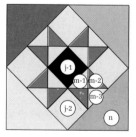

Fig B

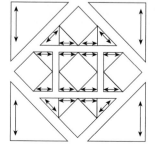

Shown in color on page 34.

Scrap quilts need some control or continuity to make them work. In this quilt, the borders selected became part of the controlling features of the quilt. The first border neutralized the large collection of prints and colors. The next three borders and the binding developed a color story that united the fabrics used.

Making the Sub-units for the Blocks

Because the Scrap Ohio Star Quilt has 35 different fabric pairs, it would be easy to lose track of the matching pairs if the hundreds of total pieces needed were cut at once. We suggest piecing the sub-units in sets, as they are cut. These sub-units, **Fig B** on page 40, are pieced just like the basic Ohio Star block. Refer to page 20 for more detailed directions.

For strip cutting techniques, refer to The Rotary Cutting Key with each pattern piece.

Making Sub-unit #1

The center square and triangles that compose sub-unit #1 are the same for each block. Cut all that are needed at once, and take advantage of chain-piecing this sub-unit.

1. From dark print fabric, use **Pattern j** to cut thirty-five squares for position j-1.

2. From light print fabric, use **Pattern m** to cut 140 triangles for position m-1.

3. Make thirty-five center square Sub-units #1 by sewing four light print triangles to each dark center square, **Fig C**, sewing opposite sides first. Finished sub-units should measure 4 1/4 inches square, including 1/4-inch seam allowances.

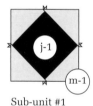

Fig C   Sub-unit #1

Making Sub-units #2 and #3

The remaining fabrics were chosen at random from assorted light, medium and dark scraps. For each block, choose the light print and the medium or dark print you will use for the star points and background. Pair these fabrics together, and work with them in sets through the block assembly step.

1. From light print fabric, use **Pattern j** to cut four squares for position j-2. Use **Pattern m** to cut four triangles for position m-3.

2. From medium or dark print fabric, use **Pattern m** to cut eight triangles for position m-2. (While you have these fabrics out, cut the corner triangles and the backing squares, see below.)

3. Make four Sub-units #2 by sewing two dark triangle[s to] each light square, **Fig D**. Two of these sub-units wil[l] used as the base for Sub-unit #3.

4. Make two Sub-units #3 by sewing a matching tria[ngle] from light fabric to each side of a Sub-unit #2, **Fig E**.

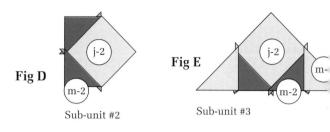

Fig D   Sub-unit #2   **Fig E**   Sub-unit #3

5. Make sub-units as above for each of the 35 blocks.

Cutting the Corner Triangles, Batting and Backing

1. From assorted medium to dark print fabrics, cut 4[0] **Pattern n** for the large corner triangles.

2. Cut thirty-five 13-inch squares of batting and asso[rted] backing fabrics. Refer to Cutting the Batting, page 5. [The] finished size of the block is 10 3/4 inches; the blocks v[ill] be trimmed to 11 1/4 inches before they are joined. ([We] even pieced some scraps and then cut the back[ing] squares.)

Assembling the Block

The Scrap Ohio Star Quilt block, **Fig B**, is assembled j[ust] like the basic Ohio Star block. Refer to page 20 for m[ore] detailed directions.

1. Layer the backing fabric, wrong side up, with the b[at]ting. Place Sub-unit #1 on top of the batting so that im[agi]nary diagonal lines through the center of the red cen[ter] square are exactly centered vertically and horizonta[lly] (6 1/2 inches from top, bottom, and sides).

2. Machine stitch, preferably with monofilament ny[lon] invisible thread, "in the ditch" along the original se[am] lines, through the batting and backing. Refer to page [__.] Stitching can be done on all the remaining blocks at [one] time to reduce the number of times the thread is chang[ed.]

3. Continue assembling the block by adding sub-unit[s to] opposite sides of the block, right sides together and [raw] edges even. Match seam lines and look for clues that s[ub]units are properly aligned before sewing. Open out [and] finger press each sub-unit as it is added.

4. Finish the block with the four corner triangles, sew[ing] opposite sides first.

5. Complete all thirty-five unit blocks in the same mann[er.]

Assembling the Quilt Top

. Before joining the blocks, trim each block to 11 1/4 nches square, which includes 1/4-inch seam allowances. ee Perfecting the Block Shape and Size, page 7.

. Assemble the blocks into seven horizontal rows of five locks each. Finishing strips are used to join the blocks. rom backing fabric, cut finishing strips on the length- vise grain 1 1/2 inches wide by 13 inches long. For com- lete instructions, see Quilt-As-You-Sew Block Assembly, Vith Finishing Strips, page 8.

. The horizontal rows are also joined together with fin- shing strips, page 8. Cut finishing strips 1 1/2 inches vide by 57 inches long.

Vhen the quilt interior is completed, it should measure 4 1/4 inches by 75 3/4 inches, including 1/4-inch seam llowances.

Adding the Borders

The first quilt border is 2 inches wide finished. Cut 2 1/2-inch wide strips from light beige print fabric for the first border.

The second quilt border is 2 3/4 inches wide finished. Cut 3 1/4-inch wide strips from medium rose print fabric for the second border.

The third quilt border is 3 1/4 inches wide finished. Cut 3 3/4-inch wide strips from dark rose print fabric for the third border.

The final quilt border is 4 1/2 inches wide finished. Cut 5-inch wide strips from dark green print fabric for the final border.

Please read Adding Borders and Binding, page 9. Also see the diagram of the completed quilt, **Fig A** on page 40.

Finishing the Quilt

A 5/8-inch French-fold binding fin- ishes the quilt. Please refer to page 12 for details.

Back of Scrap Ohio Star Quilt

Country Mini Wall Hanging

A wall hanging of this size could really be made in a weekend regardless of the method used. I thought the clean, crisp look that the Quilt-As-You-Sew technique provides, with no visible surface quilting, would enhance the design and texture of the fabric. Surface quilting in the conventional manner might have distracted from the fabrics.

APPROXIMATE SIZE:

32 1/2 inches by 32 1/2 inches

BLOCK SIZE:

7 3/4 inches square

MATERIALS REQUIRED:

1/2 yd of assorted green fabrics, including pieced border
1/4 yd of assorted very dark green fabrics, including
  pieced border
3/4 yd of assorted red fabrics, including pieced border and
  French-fold binding
1/2 yd of assorted camel fabrics, including pieced border
1 1/2 yds of backing fabric, including finishing strips
1/4 yd of dark camel fabric for border, cut crosswise and
  pieced
1/4 yd of checked fabric for border, cut crosswise and
  pieced
1 1/2 yds of cotton batting

PATTERNS REQUIRED:

Use **Patterns o**, **p** and **q**, pages 53 to 61.

Selecting the Fabric

Many quilt shops merchandise ten or twelve "fat eight of fabric together. I frequently buy these sets because I l scrap quilts, and a little bit of fabric goes a long w Recently I went to a shop that had just gotten an entire c lection of the new "Mumm's the Word" fabrics. They cut small pieces of each fabric and put them in pre rolls. I couldn't resist—they seemed perfect for this m wall hanging I had plannned, **Fig A**. That also expla why there is no piece longer than 11 inches!

Fig A

Realistically, only two fabrics of each color could ha provided enough variety, but I always prefer more to le When selecting fabrics for this project, color placement much more important than a wide assortment of fabri However, if you also like to buy those little fabric coll tions, study the photograph to get a feeling for the num and use of so many prints.

The block diagram, **Fig B**, is shaded to generally repres the fabrics in the photographed quilt. The letters cor spond to the pattern letters; number designations behin letter may mean either a fabric variation or a grainline/c ting difference. Although directions are written for photographed quilt, an empty exploded block with gra line indicators is included in **Fig B**, so that fabric substi tions can be made easily.

To help you decide on fabrics and positions, rough shapes to represent the stars and background pieces available, use a design board to position your fabrics, a stand back to study the effect. Move fabrics until you satisfied. After you have finished this planning proce there is plenty of time to worry about cutting accura pieces unless you have a very limited amount of a certa fabric.

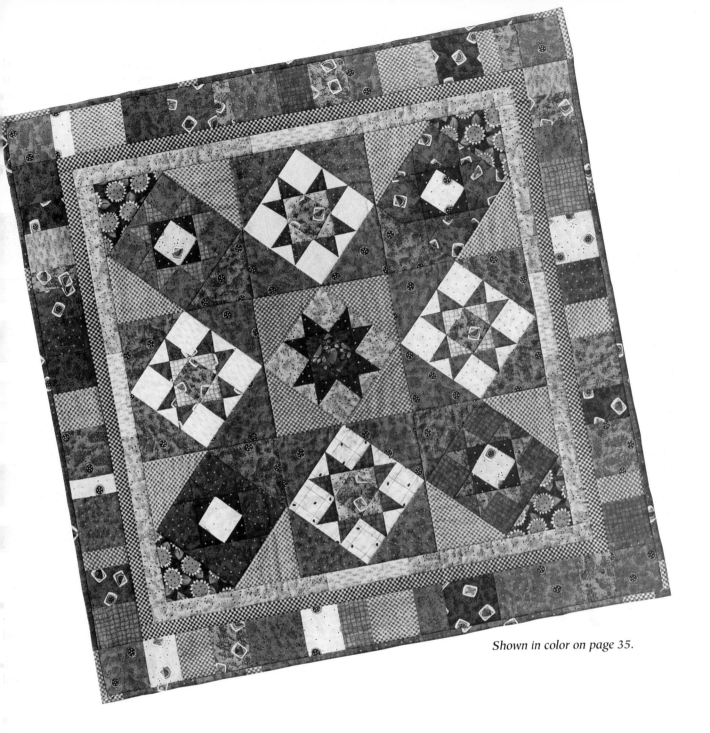

Shown in color on page 35.

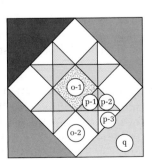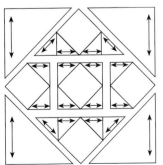

Fig B

Cutting the Fabric

For strip cutting techniques, see The Rotary Cutting Key, page 16. Look at the quilt photograph on page 35. We used the same fabric for each fabric position in individual blocks, but varied from block to block. You may choose to use random fabrics within each block to achieve a scrappier look.

1. From assorted green fabrics, use **Pattern o** to cut four squares for position o-1. Use **Pattern p** to cut thirty-two triangles for position p-2. Cut twenty of **Pattern q** for the large corner triangles (make twelve dark green and eight medium green).

2. From very dark green fabric, use **Pattern o** to cut one square for position o-1. Use **Pattern p** to cut twenty triangles for position p-1 and eight triangles for position p-2. Cut four of **Pattern q** for the large corner triangles.

3. From assorted red fabrics, use **Pattern o** to cut sixteen squares for position o-2. Use **Pattern p** to cut the following: thirty-two triangles for position p-2, and sixteen triangles for position p-3. Cut twelve of **Pattern q** for the large corner triangles (make eight dark red and four medium red).

4. From assorted camel fabrics, use **Pattern o** to cut the following: four medium camel squares for position o-1, and twenty light camel squares for position o-2. Use **Pattern p** to cut the following: sixteen medium camel triangles for position p-1, and twenty light camel triangles for position p-3.

5. Cut nine 9 1/2-inch squares of batting and backing fabrics. See Cutting the Batting, page 5. The finished size of the block is 7 3/4 inches; the blocks will be trimmed to 8 1/4 inches before they are joined.

Piecing the Sub-units

The Country Mini sub-units, **Fig B** on page 45, are pieced just like the basic Ohio Star block. Refer to page 20 for more detailed directions. Pay careful attention to the order of fabrics that you have chosen for your wall hanging.

1. Make nine center square Sub-units #1 by sewing four p-1 triangles to each o-1 square, **Fig C**, sewing opposite sides first. Finished sub-units should measure 3 inches square, including 1/4-inch seam allowances.

2. Make thirty-six Sub-units #2 by sewing two p-2 triangles to each o-2 square, **Fig D**. Eighteen of these sub-units will be used as the base for Sub-unit #3.

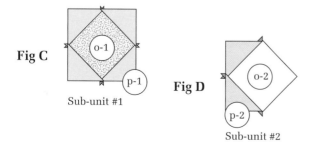

Fig C
Sub-unit #1

Fig D
Sub-unit #2

3. Make eighteen Sub-units #3 by sewing two p-3 triangl to each side of a Sub-unit #2, **Fig E**.

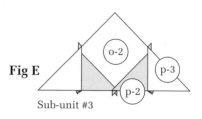

Fig E
Sub-unit #3

Assembling the Block

The Country Mini block, **Fig B,** is assembled just like t basic Ohio Star block. Refer to page 20 for more detail directions.

1. Layer the backing fabric, wrong side up, with the b ting. Place Sub-unit #1 on top of the batting so that ima nary diagonal lines through the center square are exac centered vertically and horizontally (4 3/4 inches fr top, bottom, and sides).

At this point in construction, you may wish to label ea block according to its position in the finished wall har ing (Row 1, Block A, etc.), **Fig F**. Doing so will facilita proper assembly as you sew the sub-units in place.

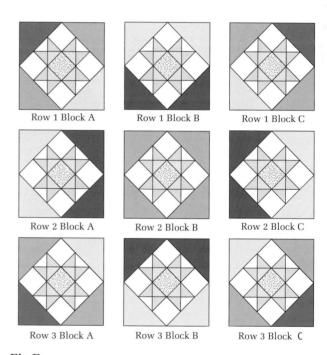

Row 1 Block A	Row 1 Block B	Row 1 Block C
Row 2 Block A	Row 2 Block B	Row 2 Block C
Row 3 Block A	Row 3 Block B	Row 3 Block C

Fig F

2. Continue assembling the block by adding sub-units opposite sides of the block, right sides together and ra edges even. Match seam lines and look for clues that su units are properly aligned before sewing. Open out a finger press each sub-unit as it is added.

3. Finish the block with the four corner triangles, sewi opposite sides first.

4. Complete all nine blocks in the same manner.

Assembling the Quilt Top

Before joining the blocks, trim each block to 8 1/4 inches square, which includes 1/4-inch seam allowances. See Perfecting the Block Shape and Size, page 7. Because the cotton batting used in this wall hanging is so dense, trim additional batting out of the side of the block, **Fig G**.

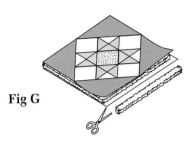

Fig G

Assemble the blocks into three horizontal rows of three blocks each. Finishing strips are used to join the blocks. From backing fabric, cut finishing strips on the lengthwise grain 1 1/2 inches wide by 9 3/4 inches long. See Quilt-As-You-Sew Block Assembly, With Finishing Strips, page 8.

The horizontal rows are also joined together with finishing strips, page 8. Cut finishing strips 1 1/2 inches wide by 25 1/4 inches long.

When the quilt interior is completed, it should measure 23 3/4 inches by 23 3/4 inches, including 1/4-inch seam allowances.

Adding the Borders

The first quilt border is 1-inch wide finished, with a 5-inch scrap of alternate camel fabric pieced into the center of each border strip. Cut 1 1/2-inch wide strips from dark camel fabric for the first border.

The second quilt border is 3/4 inch wide finished. Cut 1 1/4-inch wide strips from checked fabric for the second border.

The final quilt border is 2 1/2 inches wide finished, pieced from assorted fabrics, and accented with corner blocks from red print fabric. Cut fabric strips 3 inches wide, in lengths ranging from 1 1/4 inches to 2 1/2 inches. These fabric pieces are sewn together randomly to create the border strips.

See Adding Borders and Binding, page 9, and Adding Quilt-As-You-Sew Borders with Corner Blocks, page 11. Also see the whole quilt diagram, **Fig A** on page 44.

Finishing the Quilt

A 3/8-inch French-fold binding, pieced from assorted red fabrics, finishes the quilt. Cut fabric strips 2 1/8 inches wide, in lengths ranging from 1 1/4 inches to 4 1/2 inches. These fabric pieces are sewn together randomly to create the binding strips. Please refer to page 12 for details on adding the French-fold binding.

Good Luck in ~~Ohio Idaho~~ Iowa! Star Wall Hanging

All of the members of my family were born in the Midwest. I was raised on a farm in Iowa (that's where the tall corn grows!) that my father's family has owned since 1860. However, in 1969 my husband and I moved South and our children spent their school years in Atlanta, Georgia. Shortly after our son had finalized his plans to go to Iowa State University, the high school yearbooks arrived. Many people get confused about those state names that are short words and mostly vowels, others like to have fun with them. Regardless of the motivation or reason, the name of this quilt is the message written in our son's year book by a friend! When I saw the wonderful corn fabric by Virginia Robertson, I had to have it for an Ohio Star quilt. All of the fabrics except the sunflower are from one of Virginia's collections for Fabri-Quilt.

Good Luck in ~~Ohio Idaho~~ Iowa! is different from all the other Weekend Star quilts in this book, because the star design in this wall hanging is straight set instead of set on point, **Fig A.** Two Ohio Stars, Blocks A and B, alternate in checkerboard fashion across the quilt. Each individual block has borders added to it before being joined into the quilt top.

APPROXIMATE SIZE:
54 inches by 54 inches

BLOCK SIZE:
14 inches square

MATERIALS REQUIRED:
1/8 yd of gold print fabric
1/8 yd of orange checked fabric (including corner block~~s~~
1/4 yd of rust print fabric
1/2 yd of ecru print fabric
1/2 yd of corn print fabric
1/2 yd of sunflower print fabric
1/8 yd of brown checked fabric
1/4 yd of fabric for first border
3/8 yd of fabric for second border
1/2 yd of fabric for third border
2 1/2 yds of fabric for backing
2 1/2 yds of batting
5/8 yd of fabric for French-fold binding
Optional:
  32 or more assorted buttons, 1/2" to 7/8" diameter
  1/4 yd paper-backed fusible web

PATTERNS REQUIRED:
Use **Patterns r**, **s** and **t,** pages 53 to 61.

Key

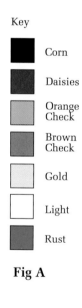

■	Corn
■	Daisies
■	Orange Check
■	Brown Check
■	Gold
□	Light
■	Rust

Fig A

Selecting the Fabric

Although three (very similar) gold print fabrics were use~~d~~ in the photographed quilt for the center square in Block and narrow borders on both blocks, yardage requiremen~~ts~~ are written as though you are using only one fabric. If yo~~u~~ prefer, purchase 1/8 yard of each of three fabrics.

The block diagram, **Fig B**, is shaded to represent the fa~~b~~rics in the photographed quilt. The letters correspond ~~to~~ the pattern letters; number designations behind a lett~~er~~

48

Shown in color on page 36.

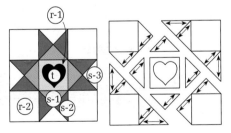

Block A

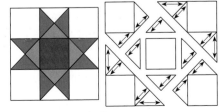

Fig B   Block B

may mean either a fabric variation or a grainline/cutting difference. Although directions are written for the photographed quilt, an empty exploded block with grainline indicators is included in **Fig B**, so that fabric substitutions can be made easily.

Cutting the Fabric

For strip cutting techniques, refer to The Rotary Cutting Key with each pattern piece.

FOR BLOCK A

1. From gold print fabric, use **Pattern r** to cut five squares for position r-1.

49

2. From orange checked fabric, use **Pattern s** to cut twenty triangles for position s-1. (Use **Pattern t** to cut four hearts to use in corners.)

3. From corn print fabric, use **Pattern t** to cut five hearts for the block centers. Also cut ten block border strips 2 1/2 inches wide by 10 1/2 inches long, and ten strips 2 1/2 inches wide by 14 1/2 inches long.

FOR BLOCK B

1. From sunflower print fabric, use **Pattern r** to cut four squares for position r-1. Also cut eight block border strips 2 1/2 inches wide by 10 1/2 inches long, and eight strips 2 1/2 inches wide by 14 1/2 inches long.

2. From brown checked fabric, use **Pattern s** to cut sixteen triangles for position s-1.

FOR BLOCKS A AND B

1. From rust print fabric, use **Pattern s** to cut seventy-two triangles for position s-2.

2. From ecru print fabric, use **Pattern r** to cut thirty-six squares for position r-2. Use **Pattern s** to cut thirty-six triangles for position s-3.

3. From gold print fabric, cut eighteen block border strips 1 inch wide by 9 1/2 inches long, and eighteen strips 1 inch wide by 10 1/2 inches long.

4. Cut nine 15 1/2-inch squares of batting and backing fabrics. See Cutting the Batting, page 5. The finished size of the block is 14 inches; the blocks will be trimmed to 14 1/2 inches before they are joined.

Making Block A

APPLIQUÉING AND PIECING THE BLOCK CENTER

1. Appliqué or fuse a heart onto the center square for each block.

2. Layer the backing fabric, wrong side up, with the batting. Place the center square on top of the batting so that it is exactly centered vertically and horizontally.

3. Stitch and flip the four orange checked triangles in position, sewing opposite sides first, **Fig B**. Open out and finger press each triangle as it is added.

PIECING THE SUB-UNITS

The remaining *Good Luck in ~~Ohio~~ ~~Idaho~~ Iowa!* sub-units, **Fig B**, are pieced just like the basic Ohio Star sub-units #2 and #3. Refer to page 20 for more detailed directions.

1. Make twenty Sub-units #1 by sewing two rust triangles to each ecru square, **Fig C**. Ten of these sub-units will be used as the base for Sub-unit #2.

Fig C

Sub-Unit #1

3. Make ten Sub-units #2 by sewing two ecru triangles to each side of a Sub-unit #2, **Fig D**.

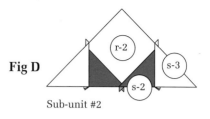

Fig D

Sub-unit #2

ASSEMBLING THE BLOCK

The *Good Luck in ~~Ohio~~ ~~Idaho~~ Iowa!* Ohio Star block, **Fig** on page 49 is assembled in a straight set. The sub-units are added stitch-and-flip, but in a different direction from the basic Ohio Star.

1. Assemble the block by adding sub-units to opposite sides of the block, right sides together and raw edges even, **Fig B**. Match seam lines and look for clues that sub-units are properly aligned before sewing. Open out and finger press each sub-unit as it is added. The Ohio Star should measure 9 1/2 inches square, including 1/4-inch seam allowances.

2. Add the first narrow border to each block. Refer to Adding Borders and Binding, page 9. For Block A, border strips will be added to the top and bottom of the block first, and then to each side, **Fig E**.

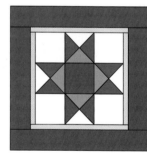

Block A   Block B

Fig E

3. Add the second border to each block in the same manner.

4. Complete all five blocks in the same manner.

Making Block B

The four Blocks B are assembled just like Block A, except Block B has no center appliqué, and the border strips are added in reverse order. When adding borders to Block B, border strips are added to the sides of the block first, and then to the top and bottom, **Fig E**. Adding the borders to the blocks in this manner avoids distracting seam lines in the completed quilt. It also makes it easy to join the blocks without finishing strips.

Joining the Blocks without Finishing Strips

When there is not a machine stitch that goes all the way to the edge of the batting on one or more edges of the block, it is possible to join the blocks without finishing strips. In this quilt, the A blocks do not have a seam going to the edge of the sides of the block. That will allow you to easily join the rows horizontally without finishing strips.

Before joining the blocks, trim each block to 14 1/2 inches square, which includes 1/4-inch seam allowances. Cut away the batting corner. See Perfecting the Block Shape and Size, page 5.

Assemble the blocks into three horizontal rows of three blocks each.

Beginning with the first two adjacent blocks in Row 1, place the Block A face down on the face up center block. Make sure block centers match. Pull back the top layer of fabric, which is the backing for Block A. Stitch through the remaining five layers of fabric and batting, **Fig F**. Join all the blocks in the first row in this manner before proceeding.

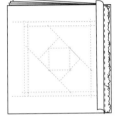

Fig F

Trim away the excess batting in the seam allowances.

Secure the loose edges of backing in each row. Working from the under side with the folded edge toward you, press under the edge of the backing 1/4 inch, so that it is even with the stitching line where the blocks were sewn together, **Fig G**. Slip stitch the folded edge in place directly on top of the seam line, using the seam as an "anchor" for the stitching.

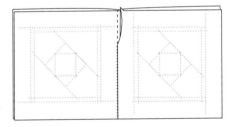

Fig G

If the blocks were trimmed accurately, (see Perfecting the Block Shape and Size, page 5), the seam allowances will be exactly 1/4 inch. There is a tendency to feel that the backing is too loose when working from the underside to secure the loose edge, and to turn under more than a 1/4-inch seam allowance. Don't! Turning under more than 1/4 inch will create a ripple on the top side of the quilt block.

Join the blocks in each horizontal row in this manner.

Joining the Rows

It was easy to sew the blocks together and finish the backs because there was no stitching that held the three layers of each block together near the edge of the blocks. That changed when the blocks were put together, so the rows can not be assembled in the same way. Instead, the horizontal rows are joined together with finishing strips, page 8. Cut finishing strips 1 1/2 inches wide by 44 inches long.

When the quilt interior is completed, it should measure 42 1/2 inches by 42 1/2 inches, including 1/4-inch seam allowances.

Adding the Borders

The first quilt border is 1 inch wide finished. Cut 1 1/2-inch wide strips of brown check for the first border.

The second quilt border is 1 1/2 inches wide finished. Cut 2-inch wide strips for the second border.

The third quilt border is 3 inches wide finished, accented with corner blocks. Cut 3 1/2-inch wide strips for the second border and 3 1/2-inch squares for the corner blocks.

See Adding Borders and Binding, page 9, and Adding Quilt-As-You-Sew Borders with Corner Blocks, page 11. Also see the whole quilt diagram, **Fig A** on page 48.

Finishing the Quilt

1. Position the four heart appliqués between the quilt blocks. Appliqué or fuse the hearts in place between quilt blocks, and sew the buttons in position, **Fig A**.

2. A half-inch French-fold binding finishes the quilt. Please refer to page 12 for details on adding the French-fold binding.

Variation— Full Size Good Luck Star Quilt

When you take away all the corn, wheat and sunflowers, it seems more appropriate to just call this pattern the Good Luck Star. A full-size quilt can be made with thirty-five blocks, set five by seven, with 6-inch borders on three sides, **Fig A.**

Fig A

APPROXIMATE SIZE:
82 inches x 104 inches

BLOCK SIZE:
14 inches square

MATERIALS REQUIRED:
2 yds of blue fabric
1 3/8 yds of white fabric
2 yds of purple fabric
2 1/8 yds of hot pink fabric
1 1/4 yds of border fabric for 3 border pieces;
   1 3/4 yds for optional 4th top border
8 yds of fabric for backing
8 yds of 48-inch wide roll batting or King Size
   packaged batt
7/8 yd of fabric for French-fold binding

PATTERNS REQUIRED:
Use **Patterns r, s, u** and Rotary Cutting Key, page 61, for **v**.

Cutting the Fabric

For strip cutting technique, refer to the Rotary Cutting Key with each pattern piece.

For Block A - make eighteen
1. From pink fabric, use **Pattern r** to cut eighteen squares for position r-1. Also, cut block border strips 1 inch wide by 9 1/2 inches long and thirty-six strips 1 inch wide by 10 1/2 inches long.

2. From blue fabric, use **Pattern s** to cut 144 triangles for position s-2.

3. From white, fabric, use **Pattern r** to cut seventy-two squares for position r-2. Use **Pattern s** to cut seventy-two triangles for position s-1 and seventy-two triangles for position s-3.

4. From purple fabric, cut thirty-six block border strips 1 1/2 inches wide by 10 1/2 inches long and thirty-six strips 2 1/2 inches wide by 14 1/2 inches long.

5. Cut eighteen 15 1/2 inch squares of batting and backing fabric. See Cutting the Batting, page 5. The finished size of the block is 14 inches; the blocks will be trimmed to 14 1/2 inches before they are joined.

For Block B - make seventeen
1. From pink fabric, use Rotary Cutting Key for **v**, page 61, to cut seventeen center squares.

2. From blue fabric, use **Pattern u** to cut sixty-eight corner triangles.

3. Cut seventeen 15 1/2 inch squares of batting and backing fabric. See Cutting the Batting, page 5. The finished size of the block is 14 inches; the blocks will be trimmed to 14 1/2 inches before they are joined.

Making Block A

The Good Luck Star block is pieced just like Block A of *Good Luck in ~~Ohio Idaho~~ Iowa!* block on page 50 (without the center appliqué). Make eighteen of Block A.

Making Block B

Center a pink 10 3/8 inch square diagonally on the batting and backing. Add blue corner triangles to the square, stitch and flip. Make seventeen of Block B.

Joining the Blocks

Assemble the blocks in the horizontal rows without finishing strips. Assemble the rows with finishing strips. Add a 6-inch border to three sides. It is not necessary to add the fourth border to get an appropriate length, but if you prefer it for design purposes, you may. You will, however, need to purchase extra fabric if you intend to add the fourth border. Bind all four edges.

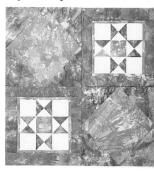

Shown in color on page 36.

Pattern Pieces

pages 53-61

ach of the pattern pieces in this section
f the book features a key to rotary
utting. It includes the cutting
ethods, the cut size and
rain line markings.

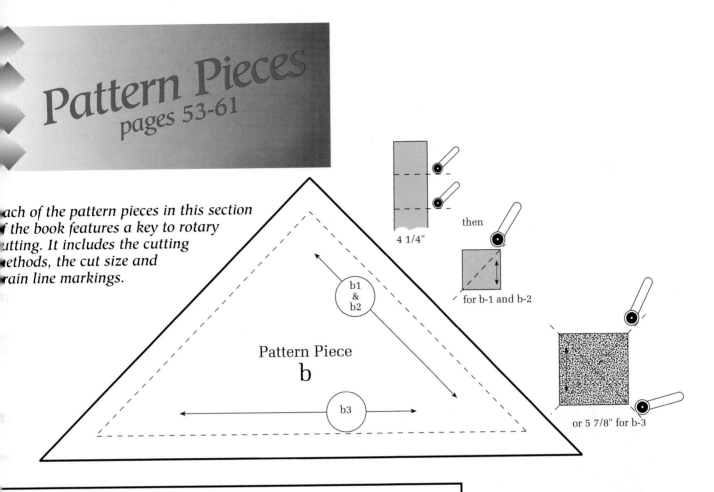

Pattern Piece
b

b1
&
b2

b3

4 1/4"

then

for b-1 and b-2

or 5 7/8" for b-3

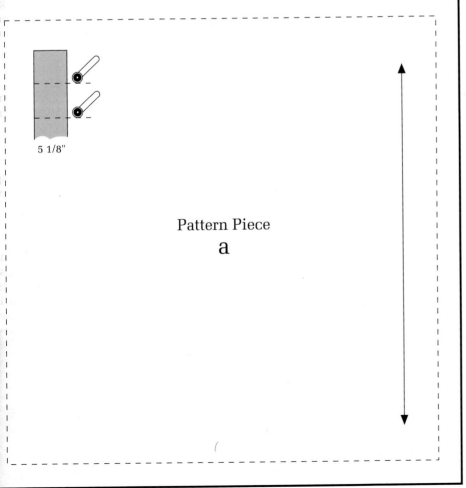

Pattern Piece
a

5 1/8"

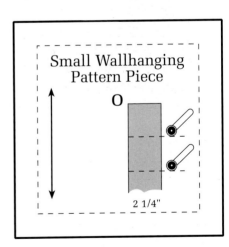

Small Wallhanging
Pattern Piece

o

2 1/4"

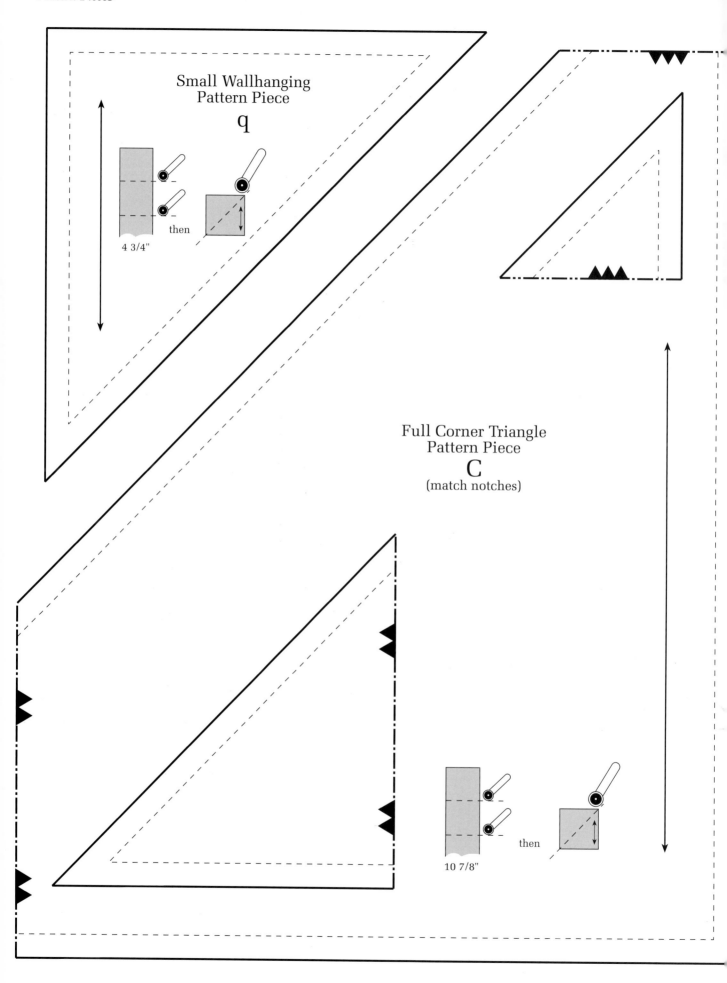

Small Wallhanging
Pattern Piece

q

4 3/4"

then

Full Corner Triangle
Pattern Piece

C
(match notches)

10 7/8"

then

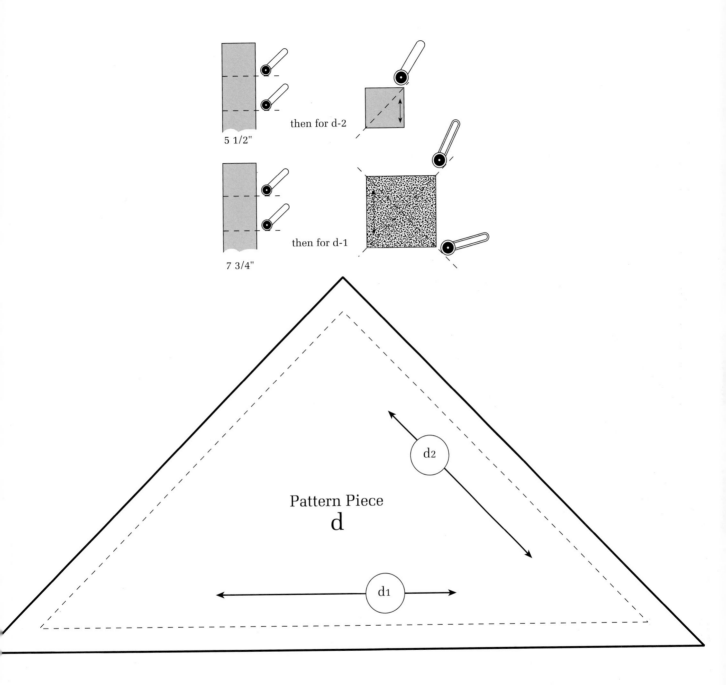

then for d-2

5 1/2"

then for d-1

7 3/4"

Pattern Piece
d

d2

d1

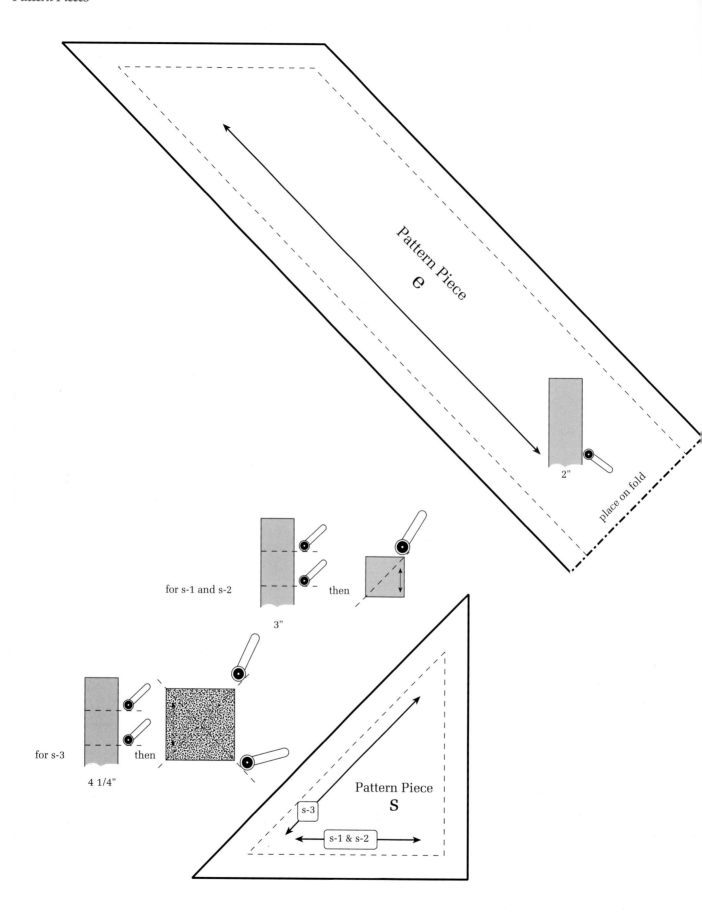

Pattern Piece
e

2"

place on fold

for s-1 and s-2

then

3"

for s-3

then

4 1/4"

Pattern Piece
S

s-3

s-1 & s-2

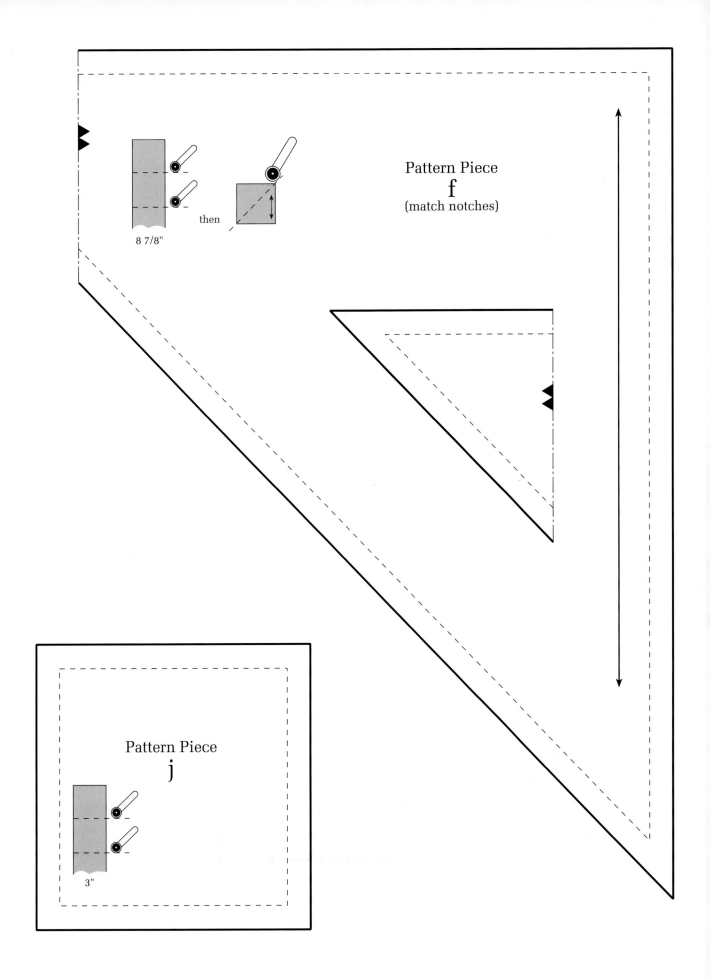

Pattern Piece
f
(match notches)

then

8 7/8"

Pattern Piece
j

3"

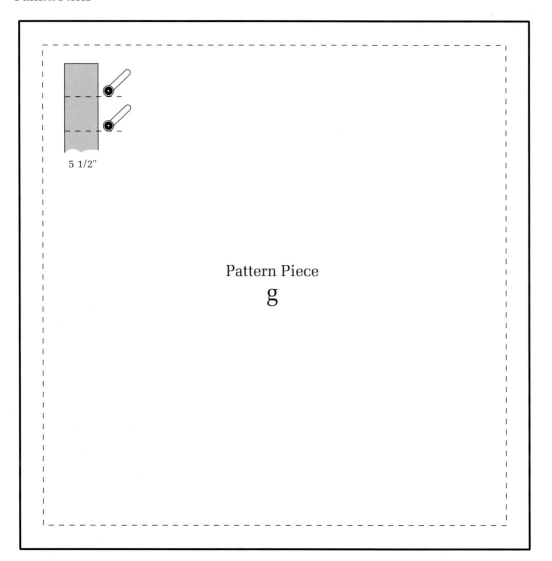

Pattern Piece
g

5 1/2"

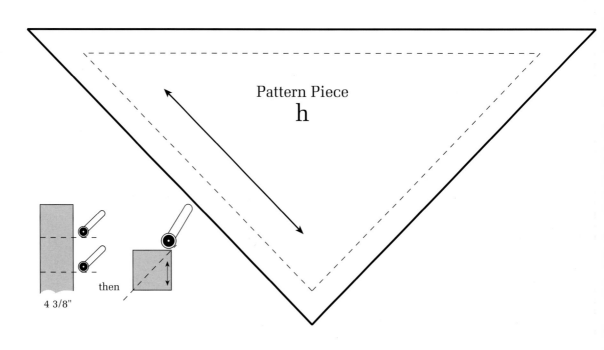

Pattern Piece
h

then

4 3/8"

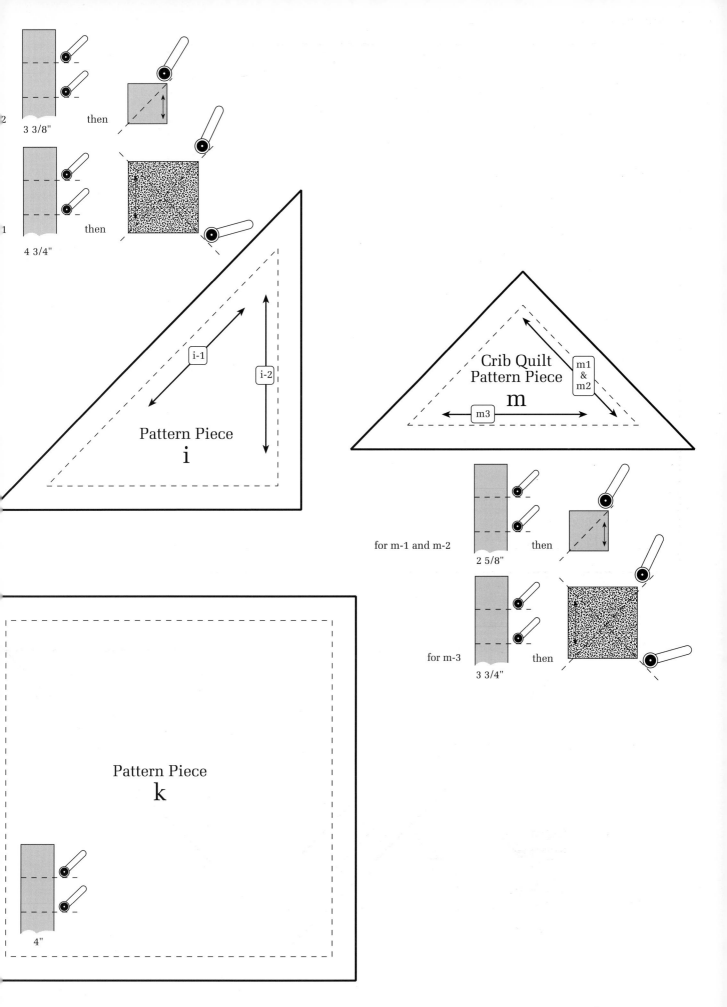

2

3 3/8"   then

1

4 3/4"   then

i-1

i-2

Pattern Piece
i

Crib Quilt
Pattern Piece
m

m1
&
m2

m3

for m-1 and m-2   then
2 5/8"

for m-3   then
3 3/4"

Pattern Piece
k

4"

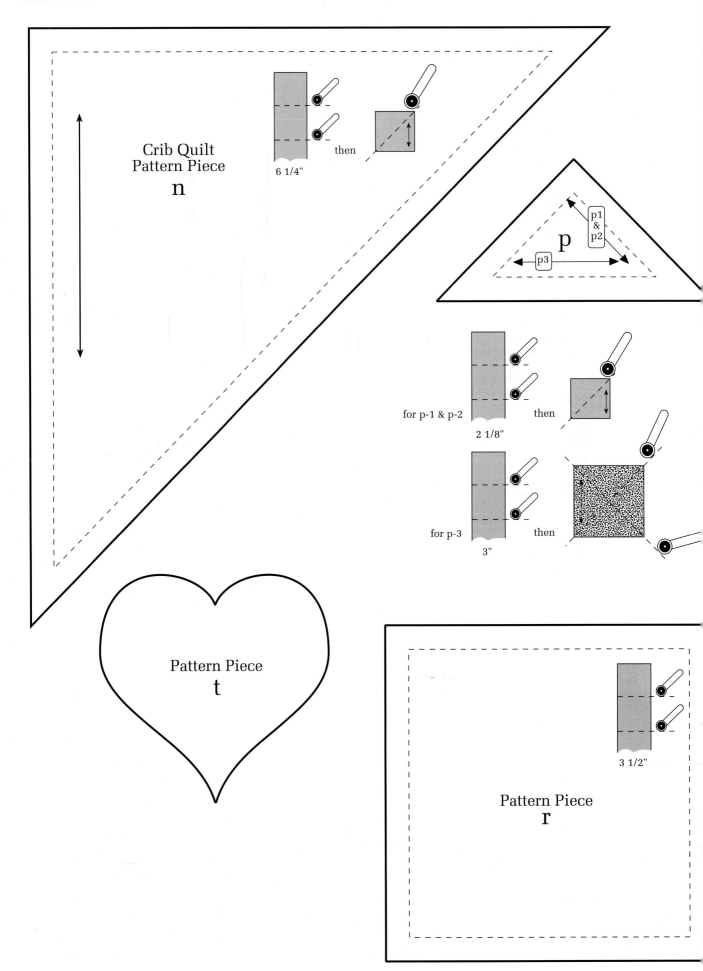

Crib Quilt
Pattern Piece
n

6 1/4"

then

p1
&
p2

p

p3

for p-1 & p-2

then

2 1/8"

for p-3

then

3"

Pattern Piece
t

3 1/2"

Pattern Piece
r